FLY FISHING
KNOTS AND
CONNECTIONS

FLY FISHING KNOTS AND CONNECTIONS

LEFTY KREH

THE LYONS PRESS
Guilford, Connecticut
An imprint of The Globe Pequot Press

The Lyons Press is an imprint of The Globe Pequot Press.

10 9 8 7 6 5 4 3 2

Printed in China

ISBN 1-59228-311-X

Frontispiece: *Bus Bergman ties a knot on the Babine River in British Columbia.*

Cover photograph by Tom Montgomery.

Color photography by :
        R. Valentine Atkinson/Frontiers
        (pages 12, 36/37, 58, 68, 88, 105)
        Tom Montgomery (pages 2, 6, 44/45, 102, 112/113)
        Sam Talarico (pages 83, 93)

Illustrated by Rod Walinchus, Livingston, Montana.

Library of Congress Cataloging-in-Publication Data is available on file.

CONTENTS

INTRODUCTION

Fly fishermen need to know more about how to tie knots and rig their tackle than do anglers using spinning or plug casting tackle. There are a variety of reasons why. Spin and plug casting tackle differs considerably from fly-fishing gear. When tossing bait, sinkers, or lures on spin and plug gear, the weight drags a uniform diameter line to the target, while in fly casting the line is the weight that transports the fly.

Most fly lines being manufactured today average in length between 80 and 105 feet. That is not nearly long enough to keep a large escaping fish under control. For that reason, a longer and thinner line, called "backing", is normally attached to the rear end of the fly line and the backing is then connected to the reel spool. To the front end of the fly line is attached a leader, to which is attached a tippet, to which is attached, in turn, the last component in a typical fly-fishing rig, the fly. These leader-line, leader-tippet, and tippet-fly connections can be constructed in many ways, depending upon the weight, density, and size of the line, leader, tippet and fly. For example, it's obvious that how you would attach a small dry fly to a fragile monofilament tippet would greatly differ from how you would connect a large sailfish fly to a heavy bite leader.

In making these observations, I am not saying that fly fishing knots and connections are especially complicated or dif-

◄ *Catching a rainbow trout in the back country of Grand Teton National Park, Wyoming.*

ficult to learn; or that you must master them all to be a successful angler. I know some people, for example, who have all their connections tied by their local fly shop, and who rely on their guide to tie most of their knots. But, to be regarded as an experienced and serious fly fisherman — and there's a bit of self-respect involved here too, I think — you should learn how to make the essential knots and connections that are required in this game. If you are fishing alone and your tippet breaks, you should know how to replace that tippet. If you fish for barracuda or bluefish, you should be able to connect a short length of bite leader of either braided or solid wire. If you are a trout fisherman, you should know the most effective ways to change your tackle when you switch from a dry fly to a nymph. These are just a few examples of the basic needs you will encounter while fly fishing. Being able to handle a few problems will alleviate the embarrassment of having to ask friends for help. And, there is a certain enjoyment in knowing how to modify your tackle or take care of immediate needs. Simply stated, it makes you independent, not having to rely on others.

Because there are special terms that are associated with rigging tackle and tying knots and connections, I have included a simple glossary. Look it over, and if any of the words are foreign to you, it may pay to familiarize yourself with them.

Bernard "Lefty" Kreh
Hunt Valley, Maryland

GLOSSARY

Arbor — The axle between the two inner sides of a reel spool.

Backing — The thinner line that is attached to the rear of a fly line, allowing the angler to let a fish run a long distance.

Bite Leader or Bite Tippet — A short length of leader between the fly and tippet that prevents sharp-toothed fish from severing the leader. It can be constructed from either heavy monofilament or from wire. It is commonly called a "shock leader" or "shock tippet," but "bite tippet" more accurately describes its function, and is to be preferred.

Braided Leader Material — A hollow-core line constructed from a lot of very tiny strands of monofilament that are braided together. It is used to attach butt sections of leaders to fly lines, such as a shooting line when using shooting tapers and for other connections to fly lines or leaders.

Butt Section — The rear portion of a leader.

Cyanoacrylate Glue — A modern glue that is extremely strong. Some cyanoacrylate glues are not waterproof. Zap-A-Gap makes one that is. In the text I will refer to Zap-A-Gap where a cyanoacrylate glue is being used. It's available in fly shops, hardware stores, and hobby shops.

Dacron (Micron) — A special type of fishing line with a hollow core that is braided. It has extremely poor knot strength but high tensile strength. Micron is a competing commercial variation of Dacron and nowadays the two words are used interchangeably. Both are used a great deal for backing.

Double Line — This refers to folding a line end over so that two strands are being used.

Double Taper Fly Line — A fly line that has a long level mid-section and has the same taper configuration on each end.

Fly Line — Any line that is used as a weight to cast a fly.

Goop — A commercial name for a glue in a tube that is highly useful to fly fishermen. There are other similar brand names of approximately the same composition. To simplify things, I'll use the name Goop. Such glues are available in fly shops and hardware stores.

Level Fly Line — A fly line of the same continuous diameter.

Level Leader — A leader of a single uniform strand.

Loop — Refers to any situation when a line is folded back on itself to form a loop.

Loop-to-Loop — Refers to connecting two loops together.

Mid-Section — This refers to the middle portion of a leader or, sometimes, a fly line.

Monofilament — A single strand of nylon monofilament (I may sometimes refer to it in the text as "mono").

Pliobond — A commercial name for a rubber-based glue that has been used for generations by fly fishermen. It is widely available in most fly shops.

Shock Leader — See "*bite tippet*" above.

Shooting Line — A light line of thin diameter which is attached between a shooting head and line backing.

Shooting Taper — Commonly called a *shooting head*, it is shorter than a conventional fly line. Its rear end is attached to shooting line. Relatively speaking, a shooting head is much heavier than the shooting line, and the heavier weight of the shooting head serves to propel the lighter shooting line at a higher velocity along the path of the cast, allowing the angler to obtain greater distance on the cast. Its commercial designation is ST (shooting taper).

Spool — Part of the reel that holds the backing and fly line.

Standing End — This is the longer or main portion of a line or leader. The term is used when describing how to tie knots.

Tag End — This refers to the very end of the line or leader being used to construct a knot.

Tapered Leader — A leader constructed of varying diameters of monofilament. It is thickest where it is connected to the fly line and gradually diminishes in diameter down its length to its end where it is connected to the fly. Knotless tapered leaders are also available commercially.

Tippet — This is the weakest or thinnest portion of any leader.

Turn — This is one circling or revolution with a line.

Weight-Forward Fly Line — A fly line designed so that the majority of the rear portion is level and thinner than the forward part which is much larger. It has a back and front taper. A weight-forward line permits most anglers to make longer distance casts than can be made with a double taper.

Wire (Braided) — Tiny strands of wire (usually stainless steel) that are twisted into a braid and used as a bite leader.

Wire (Solid) — Solid stainless steel leader wire. It was developed for trolling lures offshore, but is used a great deal in fly fishing where sharp-toothed fish are encountered.

Wrap — See "*turn.*"

OVERLEAF: *A fly fisherman casting on the Sacramento River in Northern California.*

CHAPTER ONE

TYING THE NINE ESSENTIAL KNOTS

If you fish exclusively for trout, you will need only a few necessary knots to participate in your sport. And, if you also fish for bass, you'll need probably only one or two more. But, if you want to fish for every species in fly fishing, from small brook trout in a beaver pond to giant tarpon on the saltwater flats, then there are nine knots that you will have to learn. Admittedly, there are other knots and connections worth knowing. But the nine knots I will be discussing will let you actively participate in your sport.

KNOT TYING FUNDAMENTALS

Before discussing these essential nine knots, as well as the many facets of knot building and rigging tackle (which I will refer to frequently in the text), I would like to go over a few fundamentals of good knot tying.

1) *Close all knots securely*. It must be emphasized that the most important factor in building goods knots — whether tying a two-inch hawser to secure a ship to the dock, or knotting a fragile 8X-leader tippet to a #22 dry fly — *is that no knot breaks until it begins to slip*. A poorly designed knot that has

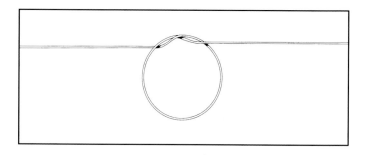

Overhand Knot

been closed very firmly will not fail as quickly as a well-designed knot that has not been closed securely.

2) *Keep knots well lubricated.* Lubricating monofilament helps better secure a knot, so it is critical you do it correctly. You can use spittle or water as lubrication. Silicone or some other slippery substance is not advised. Use of the latter will certainly allow you to close the coils easier, but under stress these materials may allow the tag end to slither through the knot, resulting in a lost fish.

3) *Check the labels on glue.* There are special glues on the market that are specially designed to be used on nylon monofilament to enhance knot strength. For example, Dupont makes a good one called "Lok-Knot." Keep in mind, however, that most of the cyanoacrylate glues that are often used for fly-fishing gear are not waterproof, so you'll want to avoid using these on your rig. You should only use glue that is specifically designed to be used on nylon monofilament, so be sure to check the label.

4) *Don't rely on the Overhand Knot.* A lot of fly fishermen tie an Overhand Knot in the tag end of their knots to prevent their original knot from slipping. This is a bad habit to get into. What it indicates is that the angler's original knot was a poor one or improperly closed.

5) *Follow knot-tying instructions correctly*. It is extremely important when tying a knot to follow the step-by-step instructions carefully. Especially critical is the number of turns you make around the standing line. Many tests have been conducted with machines (which of course have no opinion) to determine what the proper number of turns should be with the tag end on specific knot designs. For example, if a knot calls for four turns, and you only make three turns, then you have not made enough turns around the standing line to keep the knot from slipping. On the other hand, if you make five turns (one too many), then you may not be able to close the knot firmly enough to prevent it from slipping.

6) *Close the coils within a knot correctly*. Another important factor in making a strong knot is how well the coils within

How to Properly Close the Clinch Knot

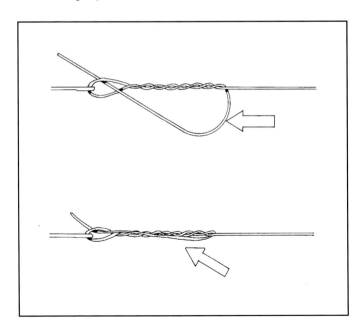

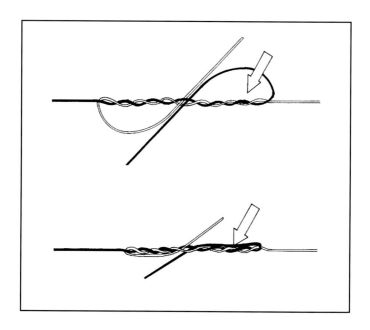

How to Properly Close the Blood Knot

the knot are closed. *Never overlap a coil*, because the point at which the coil overlaps will certainly break under severe strain. For example, when building an Albright Special, if the coils lie perfectly together, the knot will remain strong. But, if one coil crosses over another during closure, under stress this is where the knot will break. Too many fishermen are not aware that coils must come together within the knot without crossing over one another.

7) *First become proficient at tying three basic knots.* Most knots are constructed on variations of one of three knots: the Nail Knot (illustrated on pages 24-27 and pages 72-75), the Overhand Knot (illustrated on page 14), or the most often used — the Clinch Knot (illustrated on page 15). For example, the Clinch Knot forms the basis of the Blood Knot, the Uni-Knot,

the Trilene Knot, and the Improved Clinch Knot, plus a host of other knots.

Regarding the Clinch Knot, I have never seen it written or explained, but how this knot is set up *just prior to closure* is vital to producing the highest strength. Please examine the illustration of this knot carefully, so that you make the best Clinch Knot possible. And always keep in mind that *just before any Clinch Knot is closed, remove any slack in the spirals around the standing line.* This is accomplished by gently drawing on the tag end until it lies flush against the spiraled portion of the knot. .

8) *Don't attempt to tie knots in heavy monofilament with your bare hands.* Laboratory experiments have shown that if someone uses his bare hands when tying monofilament lines which test more than 15 pounds, it is impossible to secure the knot to its full potential. Use gloves, pliers, or some other device to insure proper closure.

9) *Use monofilament of the same apparent limpness.* Fly fishermen frequently need to join two sections of monofilament that are of different diameters. This occurs when building tapered leaders or when connecting bite tippets to the thinner tippet. The knots will close easier and better if you use monofilaments that are the same apparent limpness. For example, if you use some hard or stiff monofilament and try to tie it to limper mono, you'll find that the knot is very difficult to close well.

10) *Test knot strength before you add any new knot to your fly-fishing rig.* You may have been using a knot for years that you feel is a good one. Then, someone shows you one that's new to you, claiming it to be better. There is a simple test to determine which knot is better. *To test any knot properly you need to check it in two ways: with a steady pull and with a quick jerk.* To test the knot with a steady pull, take two hooks from the same box. Tie your favorite knot to one hook. Then, us-

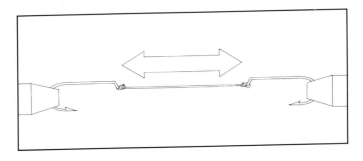

Testing Knot Strength

ing the new knot — the one that your friend has been raving about — attach it to the other end of the same length of mono. Take two pairs of pliers and grip each hook and slowly pull them apart until one breaks. Note which one broke. Repeat this test 10 times to be sure.

The other test you'll need to conduct is one using a quick jerk. Some knots, such as the Spider Hitch, are great knots on a slow, steady pull, but fail miserably if a jerk occurs. (This is why I don't recommend using the Spider Hitch.) Tie your favorite knot on another strand of mono and then tie the new knot on the other end. Grasp each end with pliers and *jerk* them until one knot fails. Note which failed. Do this 10 times. If you have *carefully* tied both knots each time, you will have a conclusive test as to which knot is stronger. I'd like to emphasize that you need to conduct a minimum of 10 tests with each method to get an idea of which knot is superior.

11) *Practice tying knots at home.* Finally, if you want to tie knots well, you need to practice them at home. I find that very few fly fishermen will do this, and that's a shame. Tying a knot over and over at home has two significant advantages: It develops good technique so that the knot is as strong as possible; and, it develops faster speed of operation, allowing the angler to make a faster connection on the water.

THE NINE ESSENTIAL KNOTS

1. Whipped Loop

This connection has a number of uses. It can be utilized to connect the leader to the fly line, backing to the fly line, a shooting head to shooting line, and for many other fly tackle rigging applications.

I much prefer the Whipped Loop to any other connection for attaching a leader to a fly line. The most significant advantage is that loops never hang up in the guides, going in or out. More importantly, there are many times at streamside when you should, or would like to, change the leader on your line, and you want to do it quickly. Let's say, for example, that you start the day fishing a small, narrow trout stream where you would need a relatively short leader. But later in the day, maybe you'll find yourself trying to fool trout on a spring creek, where you'll need to cast a longer leader to avoid spooking fish. With a Whipped Loop connection, you can quickly remove one leader and loop on the desired leader. There's simply no faster way that I know of to make this tackle change.

If you had used a Nail Knot or some other connection to attach the leader, you would have had to completely rebuild your leader. To avoid doing this, some fly fishermen use a Nail Knot to attach a short length of monofilament as a leader butt section. Then, they will make a loop in the tag end of the butt section. This procedure has never made any sense to me. The doubled and heavier monofilament of the loop tends to drown the front end of your fly line. Also, it will wear out after a while. If you want a loop, why not just install it in the fly line to begin with?

Incidentally, with a little practice, once you are ready, you can build a strong Whipped Loop in less than 30 seconds — less time than it would take to install a section of monofilament with a loop in the end.

Also, when tying any loop knot in a fly line, *it is critical that you test the loop knot after it is completed.* Insert a nail or other strong, round object in the loop. Grip the object and firmly pull on the fly line. If the loop has been improperly made, it will fail. Be sure to test the loop knot at home — not in your fishing environment.

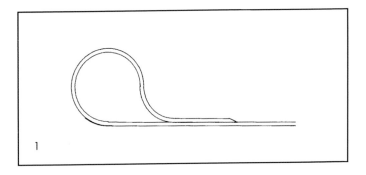

Step 1) To start, fold the fly line back on itself for about one inch to form a loop. Use a fly-tying bobbin with size-A thread (Nymo, flat-waxed nylon, Kevlar, or any strong tying thread). Insert the thread through the tube of the bobbin as you normally would. Then, remove the spool and wrap the thread around one of the bobbin legs four times before reseating the spool. The four turns will give you the tension necessary to swing the bobbin with force. If you need more thread, you will have to rotate the spool with your hands to feed the additional amount.

Step 2) Lay the tag end of the thread parallel to the tag end of the fly line and make a few turns by hand to secure the loop. Grip the loop in your right hand and the fly line (both the standing part and the tag end) in your left hand. Rotate your hands away from your body to swing the bobbin. The faster you spin it, the deeper the thread will bury itself in the outer coating of the fly line and the more secure will be the wrap.

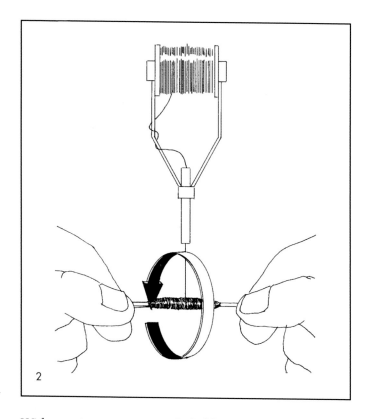

2

With practice, as you swing the bobbin you can lay each wrap against the preceding one.

Step 3) A wrap of 3/8 inch is adequate, but you might want to stretch it to 1/2 inch. Stop before you reach that distance, and taper the tag end of the fly line with a sharp knife or razor. This tapers the tag end so that when the wraps are finished, the joint will slide tangle-free in and out of the guides. To secure the wraps so they don't unravel, use a whip-finish (as described in Step 2). Many anglers prefer to lay a 10-inch piece of double mono with the loop in the direction the wraps are going. Mono testing 4 to 10 pounds is adequate. Make

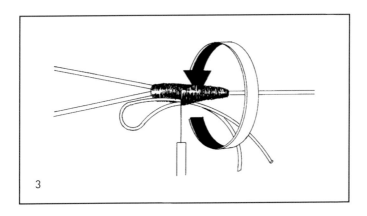

eight or 10 wraps by swinging the bobbin gently. If you swing it too hard, you won't be able to pull the mono back out.

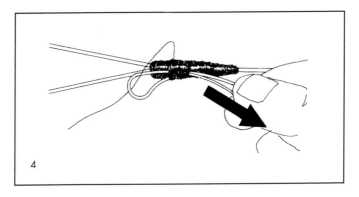

Step 4) Cut the thread coming from the bobbin and slip the tag end through the loop of monofilament. Hold the fly line and pull both tag ends of the monofilament at the same time. This will draw the thread under the wraps and secure it.

Step 5) Trim the thread at the point where it exits the wraps. Then coat the wraps with a glue or rubber-based cement (such as Pliobond). Take a moment to test the loop. Place a smooth object in the loop and pull on it with one hand while holding

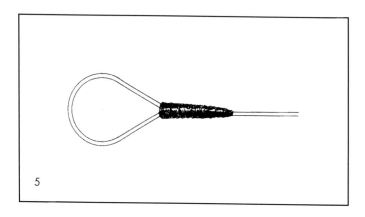

5

the fly line in the other. If the thread did not bury itself deeply enough, the loop will come out.

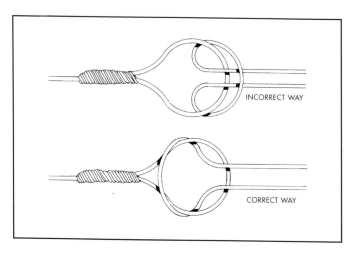

INCORRECT WAY

CORRECT WAY

When making your loop-to-loop connection, be sure that you always do so in a square knot configuration (as shown in the above illustration), never in a girth hitch configuration that will weaken the connection and form a large bump that may become jammed on the rod guides.

2. Speedy Nail Knot

This knot is used mainly to connect the leader to the fly line. It is much faster and easier to tie than the older and better known Tube Nail Knot, which is described later in the text. With a little practice, it can be made in about 10 seconds or less. One of the keys to its success is that no tube is needed. But you will need something to stiffen or hold the fly line straight while the coils are being constructed. A common needle is best. The thinner the diameter of the needle the better. When the needle is finally extracted, the smaller its diameter means the less slack remains in the coils to be removed during the tightening process.

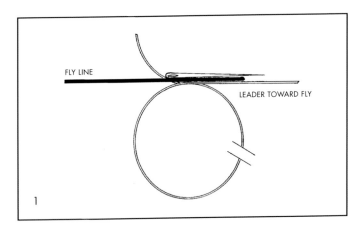

FLY LINE

LEADER TOWARD FLY

1

Step 1) Use the smallest needle possible to hold the fly line in a rigid position while you circle it with the leader. Again, the smaller the needle, the less slack will have to be removed from the Nail Knot once the needle is withdrawn.

Position the needle as shown, alongside the end of the fly line. You cannot make a Speedy Nail Knot if the leader has knots along its length — it must be a single strand of monofilament, either tapered or straight. If you are connecting a tapered leader, place the tippet, or its smallest end, alongside the needle so that it projects about an inch forward of the needle and fly line end.

The major mistake made when creating this knot is when forming the big loop shown below the needle and fly line. *You must grab the far end of the leader and bring it up and lay it as shown. Do not grab that part of the leader immediately below the needle and fly line.*

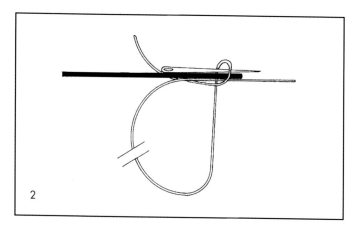

Step 2) Pinching the needle, fly line, and leader together firmly, grab the right side of the leader *within an inch* of the needle and make a full circle around the needle, fly line, and butt section of the leader.

Step 3) It is at this point that most people have a problem. You must make *all the wraps to the left* (this is the opposite direction from making wraps when using the Tube Nail Knot).

Another important consideration when making the Speedy Nail Knot is to grip the line making the circle no farther than 1 1/2 inches from the connection and *at all times keep tension on the line. If you relax, the coils you have made will spring up and spoil the knot!*

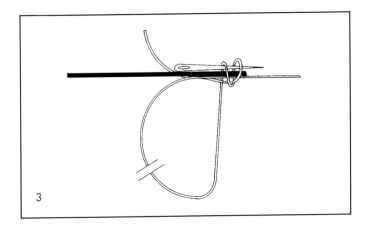

3

Also, make note that the more neatly all coils are placed one against the other, the less adjusting you will have to do when you finally close the knot.

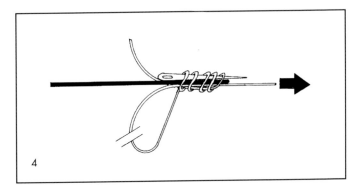

4

Step 4) Make sure that all coils you make are clenched firmly between the thumb and forefinger. When at least five coils (five to seven is what most people prefer) are made around the fly line, you can begin to close the knot. Hold the coils firmly and draw on the one-inch end that is protruding in front of the needle and fly line end. This will draw the entire leader through the coils that you made. Sometimes you may need to moisten the leader or withdraw the needle slightly to the left to allow the entire leader to be drawn through the coils.

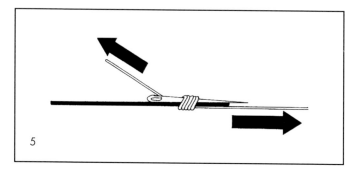

Step 5) After all of the leader has been pulled through, but before the needle is extracted, tease all coils so that they lie close together, as shown in the illustration. *Do not pull the knot too tight, or you will have trouble withdrawing the needle.*

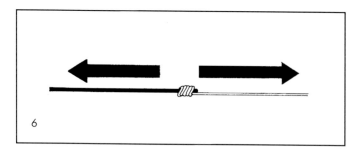

Step 6) Remove the needle and pull as tightly as possible on *both* ends of the leader. Try to bury the knot down into the coating of the fly line. Clip off the ends of the fly line and butt section so that they are flush against the coils. *Always be sure to firmly pull on the leader and fly line after the knot is completed to be sure it is intact.*

3. Surgeon's Knot and Loop

There are many fly-fishing situations where a Surgeon's Knot is the best choice for connecting two different diameters of line. Of course, it can be used to connect two lines of the same diameter, or to connect braided wire to monofilament — a method many fishermen don't realize. For many fly fishermen the Surgeon's Knot is also the preferred knot for building tapered leaders. When properly tied it has a knot strength exceeding 90 percent of the weaker of the two lines used in the connection. *I consider this to be one knot that every fisherman should know how to tie!*

However, this knot will not form properly in lines testing more than 60-pound-test. Instead, I would suggest using the Albright Knot (described on pages 35-40) when connecting lines of more than 60-pound-test to smaller lines.

The most important factor in building the Surgeon's Knot so that it retains maximum strength is that after closure *all four ends of the knot must be firmly pulled tight.*

Note in the illustrations that the solid black line is the leader, while the white line is the length that will be attached to the leader end.

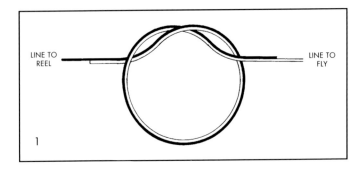

LINE TO REEL

LINE TO FLY

1

Step 1) Lay the two ends opposing each other. Placing them parallel to each other will not work. To understand this, put your hands in front of you and point the first finger of each hand at the other hand. Then, bring those fingers toward each other until the thumbs touch. This is the way the two strands should line up before making two Overhand Knots, as shown.

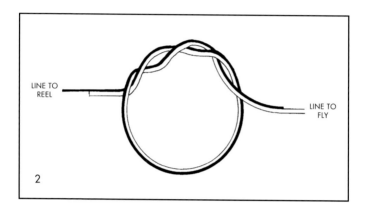

Step 2) Pass the two ends on the right through the Overhand Knot again and then lubricate. Pull all four ends tight to create the Surgeon's Knot.

Here is a really quick way to make the Surgeon's Loop. Properly constructed it is about as strong as most loops. It is not, however, as strong as a Non-Slip Mono Loop (see page 43) — the strongest of all loops.

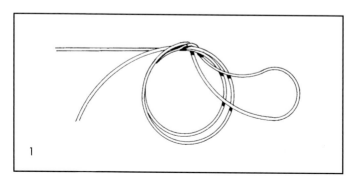

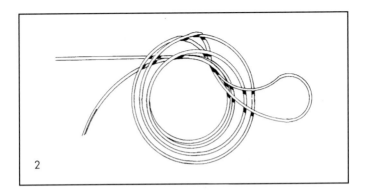

Step 1 and 2) This loop is made the same way as you would form a Surgeon's Knot. Double a single piece of leader material and then proceed to form the knot as described above.

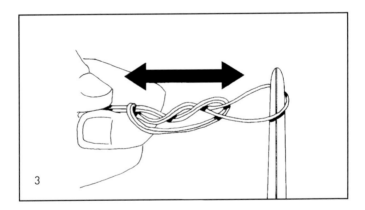

Step 3) The major difference here is how the knot is finally closed. Remember, all four ends of a Surgeon's Knot have to be pulled tight. But when making the Surgeon's Loop, the two ends of mono that form the loop are difficult to pull tight with your bare hand. So, to insure that your Surgeon's Loop is at maximum strength, insert a smooth, round object in the loop formed at the right (hemostats, pen — anything smooth and

round). Pull the tag end and then the standing end with the left hand, pulling against that force with the object you are holding in your right hand. Make absolutely sure that your hands are placed evenly apart, applying equal and firm pressure to the ends within the loop.

4. Bimini Twist

This is the most important knot that a saltwater fly fisherman can learn. It also has applications in freshwater. Whenever you want to connect a fragile line to another line and want to *retain 100 percent strength of the fragile line*, the Bimini Twist is the answer.

Many fishermen do not understand the reason why a Bimini Twist is so valuable: there are almost no other knots that offer full-line strength. If you tie another type knot to a swivel, hook, or other device, usually the knot will be weaker than the line it is tied with. The Bimini Twist is a wrapping in the line that is stronger than the actual line. And, most important, *it produces a loop — or two strands — which are used to tie your next connection.* And, since the Bimini Twist is stronger than the line, and you are tying the knot with two strands of the line, almost any knot you tie will be stronger than the main line. This is the reason why the Bimini is used throughout the fishing world, from big-game trolling to fishing with a four-pound light fly tippet.

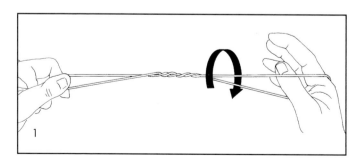

1

Step 1) Double back about 2 feet of the line end, grasp the main line with the two shortest fingers of your hand, and hold the tag end with the thumb and first finger. Insert your other hand inside the loop and rotate your hand clockwise 20 times. (Years ago this was often called the "20 times around" knot.)

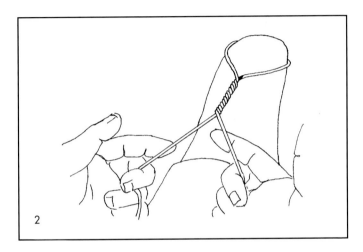

2

Step 2) Don't let the twist unwind while you slip the loop over your knee — making sure that the foot is tucked back under the knee. If the shinbone is vertical, the loop may slide off your knee. Grasp the short end in your right hand and the standing line in your left hand. *Keep tension on the line at all times or the loop will slip off the knee and the twists will unwind. Slowly* separate your hands. This will force the twists to "pack together." As the hands spread, keep the angle of the two lines in a large "V" as shown in the illustration.

Step 3) When the twists have been packed as tightly as possible, move the line in the right hand down so that it slips over the twists. *Then, re-position the line in the right hand so that it is at slightly more than a right angle to the twists. The angle at which you hold the tag end will determine if the wraps are close*

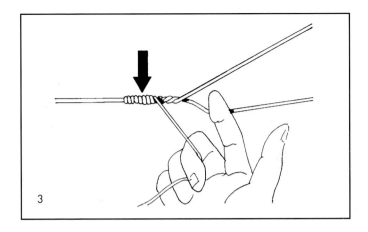

3

together or spiraled loosely. By pulling on the standing end in your left hand and feeding the tag end of the line from the right hand, you can wind the tag end around the 20 twists until they are completely covered. If the tag end doesn't wrap to the end of the twists, you can insert the finger as shown and push against the twists, which will permit you to feed the tag end until it completely wraps over all twists. This sounds more complicated than it really is.

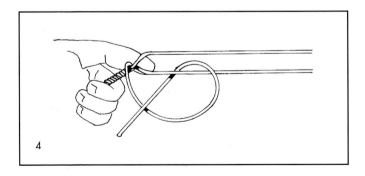

4

Step 4) Work your left hand down the standing line so that you can hold the over-wrapped twists and nothing unwinds (as shown in the illustration). Make a half-hitch with the tag end on one side of the loop. This is simply to insure that the twists don't unwind.

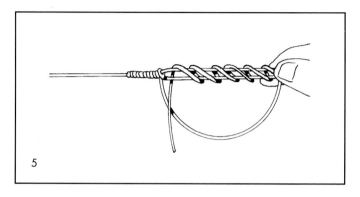

5

Step 5) Remove the loop from your knee and slip it over a small object, such as a nail or boat cleat or someone's finger. Make six half-hitches *around both sides of the loop*, as shown.

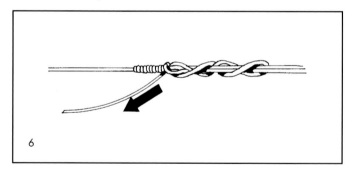

6

Step 6) Keep the loop on the nail or cleat. To secure the knot so it will never come apart, pull carefully on the tag end. Some of the half-hitches may try to jump over the knot and cause a bad snarl. As the tag end is gently pulled, stroke the half-hitches so that they close together smoothly.

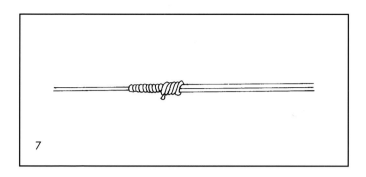

7

Step 7) Once the half-hitches have been firmly pulled together, you can clip the tag end and the Bimini Twist is completed.

5. Albright Knot

There are many knots used to connect two lines of monofilament that differ considerably in diameter. But, the most useful of these is the Albright Knot. (The Huffnagle is a modern knot that does the same thing, though this knot is more limited in use than the Albright.) *This is one of the most important knots that a fly fisherman should master.* The Albright Knot can be used to join monofilament to monofilament, monofilament to braided wire, monofilament to solid wire, a butt section to a fly line, and backing to the fly line (although there are better knots for the last two purposes). Like the Surgeon's Knot, the Albright is a versatile knot that can be used in a great many fishing situations.

When connecting monofilament to wire, or connecting monofilament of two very different diameters, I suggest using the Albright Knot with a lock, as shown in the series of illustrations that follow. Note that while the smaller line can be used as a single strand, it is often made into a Bimini Twist, with the double strands utilized to give the knot greater strength.

Overleaf: *Trout fishing on Hat Creek in California.*

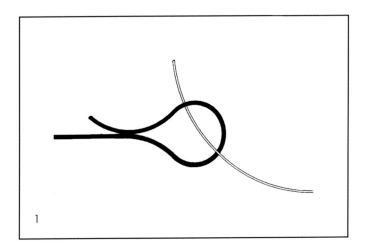

Step 1) Bend the larger line over and insert the tag end of the smaller line inside the loop as shown.

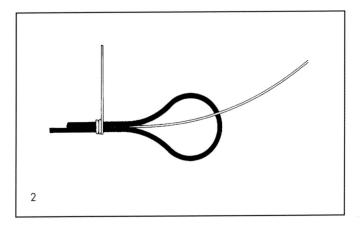

Step 2) Using the tag end of the smaller line, make at least a dozen wraps around the double portion of the wire or large line. To keep the coils in place, pinch them securely between the finger and thumb.

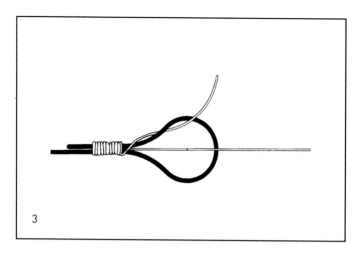

Step 3) While holding the coils securely, push the tag end through the open loop.

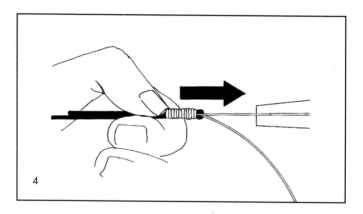

Step 4) Slide the coiled wraps forward until they are near the end of the bend in the larger line. Grasp the tag end firmly and pull it until the coils tighten. *Important: never pull on the standing line at first, or you will slide all the coiled wraps off the line and the knot will fall apart.*

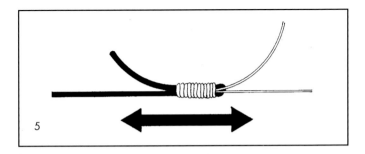

Step 5) After the tag end has been pulled tight, pull firmly on the standing end. You may have to alternate pulling on the tag end and then the standing end several times to get the knot to close securely.

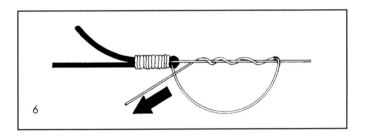

Step 6) Using the tag end, make three or four hitches around the standing line, then pull on the tag end to form a locking knot so that the Albright will never come apart.

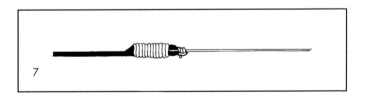

Step 7) Trim both ends flush against the knot so that it will pass through the rod guides easily.

When connecting an Albright Knot (with or without a lock) to solid wire, make the Albright Knot, and after it is finished, make a Haywire Twist (illustrated on pages 117-118) in the wire immediately below the Albright.

One of the most important factors in making an Albright is that you should never cross one wrap over the other as the knot is being built. Under great stress this is where the knot will break.

Note that in the illustration below the wire is to the left and the monofilament is to the right.

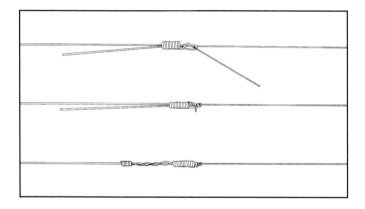

Connecting an Albright Knot to Solid Wire

Step 1) Bend the wire over as shown and make a series of wraps with the monofilament as you would with any Albright Knot.

Step 2) Close the knot securely and make the lock (as previously described).

Step 3) There are times, under stress from fighting a large fish, when the wire may slither through the monofilament. To prevent the knot from ever coming apart in this manner, you should add a Haywire Twist below the Albright. This will form a solid connection that simply won't come apart.

6. Trilene Knot

This knot isn't recommended for lines testing more than 15-pound test. But with the smaller diameter monofilament lines, it is one of the strongest knots you can use for attaching a hook to a tippet. When tied correctly, even in a fragile 7X-tippet, this knot will usually not break, although the standing line will. When properly constructed, the Trilene is superior to almost all other knots for attaching a hook to light monofilament.

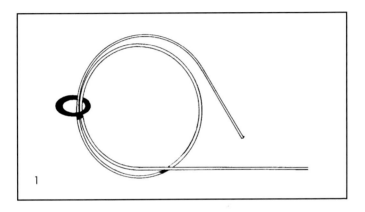

1

Step 1) Insert the tag end through the hook eye *two times.* Make sure that you have three inches of tag end to work with after the two loops have been made. *Pull* the tag end until the two loops are the same size (smaller than a dime). Larger loops will make it more difficult to close the knot.

Step 2) Make five wraps around the standing line with the tag end, and then insert the tag end through the two loops. *The knot is now ready to be closed. Do not make this like an Improved Clinch Knot as this will weaken the knot.* Simply insert the tag end through both the loops. Carefully draw the knot tight. It is important how you tighten the Trilene for full strength. Because the loops go around inside the hook two times, you may have to work the loops tight with your finger-

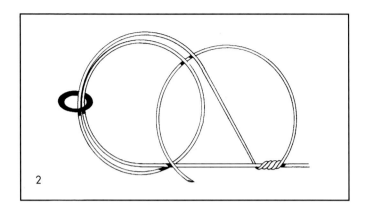

2

nail. Final closure requires that you pull firmly on both the standing and tag ends. When closed properly, this is one of the strongest single-strand knots ever invented.

7. NON-SLIP MONO LOOP

This is an old knot that I worked with for months before finally improving it. When tied properly the knot will not break. In fact, except for the Bimini Twist, this is the strongest loop knot that I have ever tested. It can be tied in any diameter line from 8X to 150-pound monofilament, as well as in braided wire. *But it is critical that it be tied correctly.* Tied correctly, it will test at full-line strength. Equally important, the *correct number of turns must be made with the tag end around the standing line*.

There are a host of fishing situations where a loop knot is desirable to a rigid connection (such as a Trilene or Improved Clinch Knot) for attaching the fly to the tippet. Popping bugs work so much better when attached so that they can swing freely on a loop. Or, anytime a heavy tippet is connected to a smaller fly, the junction between the two can stifle the action

OVERLEAF: *A day of boating on the Bighorn River, Montana.*

of the fly. Or, with heavy or bulky flies, such as the crab patterns that are now being used on permit, lifelike action can frequently be better created with a loop connection.

Some people use the Uni-Knot for this type connection. Certainly this is better than not using a loop knot at all. But the Uni-Knot is not nearly as strong as the Non-Slip Mono Loop. And, the Uni-Knot often slips down and tightens rigidly on the hook eye under fighting pressure. The Non-Slip Mono Loop retains its shape regardless of fishing conditions.

I also much prefer to make a Non-Slip Mono Loop when constructing a loop in the end of a tapered monofilament leader. (Later in the book, I'll go into how I build tapered trout leaders so that you can quickly switch — for such work the Non-Slip Mono Loop is ideal.)

This knot looks complicated, but it is really a simple operation to tie it. Just remember that you make an Overhand Knot, then pass the tag end through the hook eye, back through the Overhand Knot, make some turns around the standing line, and pass the tag end back through the Overhand Knot.

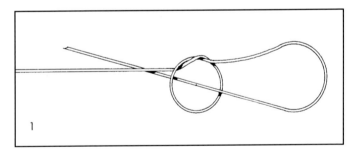

Step 1) Begin by making an Overhand Knot. *It is vital to knot strength that you have the tag end go back through the Overhand Knot on the same side it came out. If it passes through the opposite side, knot strength will be lost.*

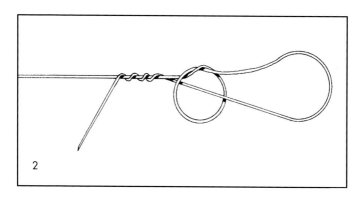

2

Step 2) Insert the tag end back through the Overhand Knot on the same side as you did the previous two times. Since you want to create a reasonably small loop, there are two things you can do at this point to create a small loop. First, you can control the size of the Overhand Knot, because the smaller the Overhand Knot, the smaller will be the loop. To end up with a small loop, after the tag end is returned through the Overhand Knot, pull the standing line until the Overhand Knot is less than 1/4-inch diameter. Then, to make the loop even smaller, hold the fly (not the standing end) and gently pull on the tag end until the Overhand Knot slides down against the hook eye. These two steps will aid in making the smallest loop possible.

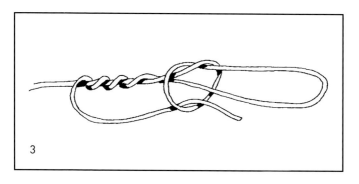

3

Step 3) It is important to make the proper number of turns around the standing line to obtain full line strength. For lines testing from 8X to 6 pounds, make *seven* turns; for those testing from 8 to 12 pounds, make *five* turns; for those testing from 15 to 40 pounds, make *three* turns; and for those lines testing 50 to 60 pounds, make *two* turns. For monofilament stronger than 60 pounds, you only need to make *one* turn.

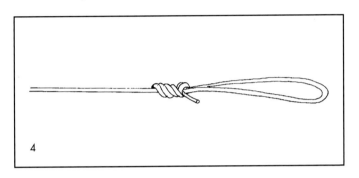

Step 4) How you close the knot is also important. You must tease the spirals of the tag end made around the standing end until they lie together (please refer to page 15 for how to properly close a Clinch Knot). Lubricate the knot. Pull on the standing and tag ends. When this has closed well, give a firm pull on the tag end, and then repeat pulling on the tag end and the standing end to insure that the knot is firmly closed.

8. George Harvey Dry-Fly Knot

There are a host of knots used to attach a tippet to a dry fly. A problem with knots that are most frequently used to attach tippet to dry flies, such as Trilene or Improved Clinch knots, is that the connection will sometimes slip off to one side, causing the fly to cock at an odd angle as it rides on the surface of the water. And that, in turn, results in refusals by trout examining the offering.

And, for dry-fly patterns tied on hooks with turned-up or turned-down eyes, the best knots are those in which the tippet enters the front of the hook eye and the knot is secured on the shank or the head wrappings. For many years the Turle Knot has been a standby for this purpose. But I prefer one that was designed by George Harvey, one of the best trout fishermen that has ever lived. The George Harvey Dry-Fly Knot is a much stronger knot. But keep in mind, *this knot should be tied only on hooks with turned-up or turned-down eyes. If tied on a ring-eye hook, it will cause the fly to run at an odd angle.*

George Harvey's knot may look complicated, but if you follow the directions you'll find it is easy to tie. You see, all you are going to do is make two circles around the standing line with the tag end, and then take the tag end through those two circles. One of the best things about this knot is that if it is tied correctly, the two loops will jump over the hook eye during closure, as shown in the illustration. If the loops won't flip over as shown, you have tied the knot incorrectly.

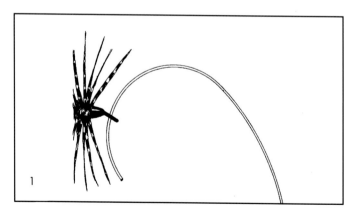

1

Step 1) Insert the end of the tippet in the front of the hook. The knot won't close properly if you insert the tippet from the rear of the hook eye.

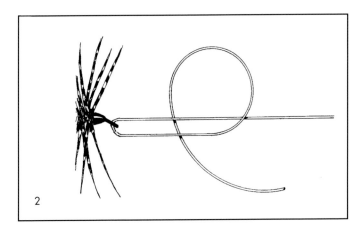

Step 2) Do not hold the hook, but clasp the two strands immediately in front of the hook eye between the thumb and the first finger. Make a *full circle* with the tag end around the standing line. You should form a circle (not a spiral such as would be made with a Clinch Knot).

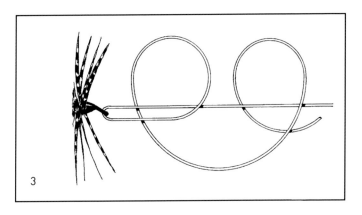

Step 3) Make another circle around the line. While the illustration shows the circles apart from each other, you should put them together (as shown in Step 4). The smaller you make the two circles, the easier it will be to close the knots. (I like to make them about 1/3 the diameter of a dime.)

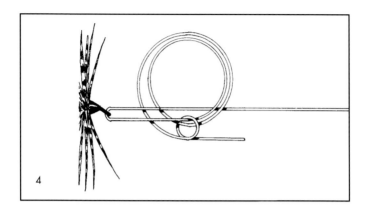

Step 4) Insert the tag end through the two formed circles, making sure that you insert it *from the front*. Never bring it through the circles from the rear. Also, be careful not to take the tag end over the standing line.

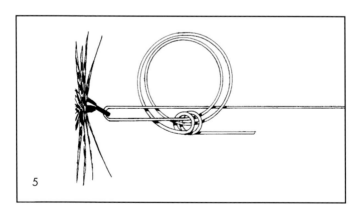

Step 5) Take the tag end through the two circles again, from the front as in Step 4.

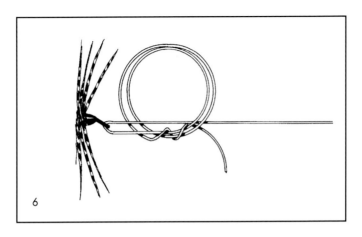

Step 6) When the knot is ready to close, it looks like this. All this time, while the knot has been forming, the thumb and the first finger are clasping the two loops in front of the fly.

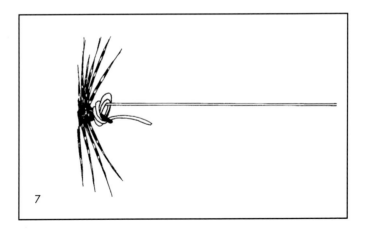

Step 7) This knot closes differently than almost any other knot. Slide the thumb and finger back over the fly so that the wraps behind the hook are exposed. *Draw slowly on the standing line, making sure that you release the tag end.*

If the knot has been tied correctly, the two loops will slide back and jump over the hook eye. If the knot was formed incorrectly, or if you held the tag end when closing the knot, the loops will not jump over the hook eye.

Step 8) To obtain full strength, complete the knot properly by teasing the tag and the standing ends until they close tightly around the hook just behind the eye. It is important on final closure that you give a firm pull on both the standing and tag ends of the knot.

9. FIGURE 8 KNOT (WITH ORVIS KNOT VARIATION)

This knot is *only* used to attach braided wire to a swivel or hook eye. It won't work with solid wire nor should it ever be tied using nylon monofilament. If you do, the knot will slip or fail miserably. But, it is an incredibly simple knot to tie in braided wire and has excellent strength.

Aside from tying it correctly, the most important factor when making the Figure 8 Knot is how tightly you draw it. *Never pull on the standing line to close the knot.* This will feed kinked line in front of the fly, causing it to wobble erratically on the retrieve. Be sure to carefully draw out all slack within the knot, pulling the tag end. That way all kinks in the line can be clipped and discarded.

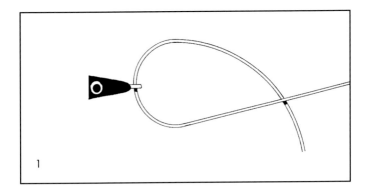

Step 1) Insert braided wire into the hook eye with the tag end away from you. Swing the tag end under the standing end.

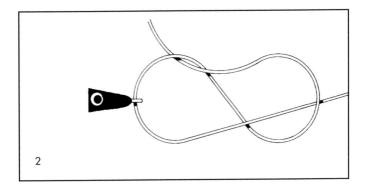

Step 2) Bring the tag end over the top and insert it in the loop immediately in front of the hook eye.

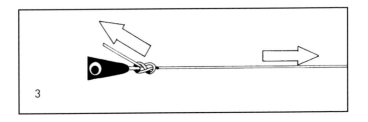

Step 3) How you close the knot is important! To close it, draw all slack from the tag end. Since this is wire, it tends to deform as it crawls through the knot during closure. You want to draw all deformed wire out through the hook eye, so it can be clipped and removed.

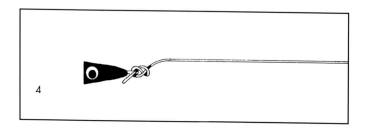

Step 4) If you pull on the standing end while closing the knot, kinked wire will be pulled in front of the hook eye, causing the fly to swim poorly on the retrieve.

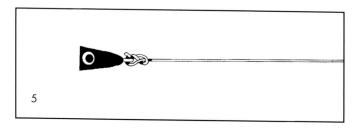

Step 5) If you pull only on the tag during closure, the wire will be straight, as shown.

As I have already mentioned, the Figure 8 Knot is wonderful for use with braided wire, but it should not be used with monofilament since it has little strength. When I am using monofilament, I'll use a variation of the Figure 8, which is the Orvis Knot. It is very high in knot strength as well as easy and quick to tie. I simply add a step to the Figure 8 to produce this knot.

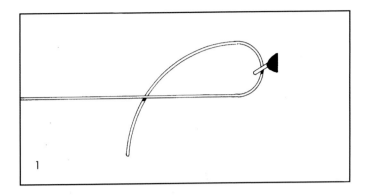

Step 1) Insert the monofilament end through the hook eye and bring the tag out and under the standing line.

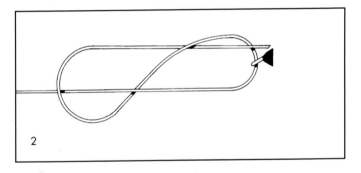

Step 2) Swing the tag end under and then over the standing end and insert it through the loop as shown.

Step 3) Pass the tag end two times around line that lies parallel to the standing line, as shown in the illustration.

Step 4) Be sure to tease the coils together (see the illustration on how to properly close a Clinch Knot on page 15).

To complete the knot, lubricate the connection and pull the tag end to partially close the knot. When it fuses loosely together, grasp the hook firmly and pull on the standing line to get a final closure on the knot.

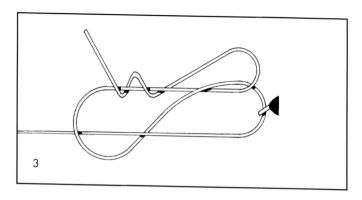

3

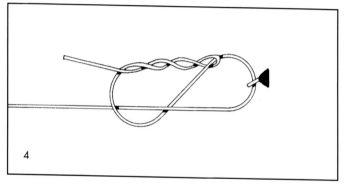

4

Armed with all of the knots that I have covered here, you can go almost anywhere and be able to effectively fly fish. But I will continue with a number of other knots and connections that will certainly make your fly-fishing life more interesting and fruitful.

Note that since this book is about the various knots and connections that are required to rig fly tackle, I am going to cover the following material where the rigging begins — at the reel spool — and proceed along the path of the rigging until its termination at the fly connection.

OVERLEAF: *Catching a trout on the Green River in Utah.*

CHAPTER TWO

BACKING TIPS AND TRICKS

BACKING TIPS

Probably no piece of fly-fishing gear is so ignored as the backing on the reel. In fact, great fish are often lost because this part of the tackle is not considered to be very important by many fly fishermen. And this does not only apply just to saltwater situations. Steelheaders often watch with dismay while their trophy fish escapes downstream, where they can't follow, only to see the end of the backing and the end of the fight. Atlantic salmon fishermen are often called upon to give more line than they want to a battling fish. And, even on very light gear, a good trout hooked in heavy water may take out more than 90 feet of fly line.

Fly lines usually range in length from about 80 to 105 feet. This is a very short run for some freshwater fish, and certainly for most saltwater species. So, to allow a fish to make long runs and exhaust itself, there has to be enough backing on the reel so that the fish you hook can be landed.

However, you can't use just any old type of backing. The kind of backing, the amount, sometimes the color, and even the combination of backings used can all play an important role in successfully catching fish.

There are a number of different types of line used for backing. Though it is rare, some people are still using nylon monofilament. This material is a poor one to use for backing because it stretches when pulled taut. If you are fighting a strong fish with mono backing, you may recover line on the reel that's in a stretched condition. With the mono in this condition, if you then reel more loose line on top of the taut mono, you will create a critical problem. That is, when the fish makes another long run, the extended line will probably reach the stretched portion of the line on the reel (which has now become thinner and has dug into the bed of line) and is likely to produce a jerk in the line that may, and often does, snap your leader.

These days, the most popular backings are Dacron (manufactured today by a number of companies) and Micron (manufactured by the Cortland Line Company), two commercially manufactured backing materials that are widely available in all fly shops. These two materials are popular because they stretch very little under stress, and both lie flat on the spool.

One of the first braided nylons to come on the market was squidding line. For many years experienced fly fishermen used this material as it worked well and lay flat on the spool. But squidding line is pretty difficult to obtain now.

When the first ultra-thin braided casting lines, such as DuPont's Kevlar, gained popularity on the market in 1993, they appeared to be a real breakthrough in fly reel backing. They are a totally new breed of lines. These lines are unlike those made of other materials (Dacron, Micron, braided nylon, or nylon) in that they have one outstanding characteristic: thin diameter for their strength. The average new braided casting line of 30 pounds has the diameter of about a 10-pound nylon monofilament line.

Fly fishermen immediately make the mistake of thinking, "Great! Since the line is so thin, I can put two or three times as much backing line on a reel as I do now for the same line test." However, there are some drawbacks to these lines.

First, I believe if you use any of these braided lines testing *less than 30 pounds* for backing you will encounter troubles. Such lines testing less than 30 pounds are so thin that they tend to dig into the backing, causing the same kind of problems associated with nylon monofilament, as I have discussed above. And, many of these lines are round and very slick. If you do not level-wind the line back onto the reel spool *very carefully*, as you recover it while fighting a fish, the line will pile up higher on one side of the spool, creating a greater tendency for the line to tumble into a disastrous mess. Also, when fighting very large fish, these very thin lines can cut your fingers.

Second, you are going to need (and need to learn) special knots to tie most of these newer braided casting lines. *Conventional knots usually are poor performers with these lines.*

Third, keep in mind that when using these new braided lines for backing on fly reels, the most important factor in getting good performance is *how the line is positioned on the spool.* Even when using 30-pound-test line which has such a thin diameter, you must make sure that all backing when installed on the reel is put on as firmly as possible. *I use a glove to put tension on the line as I reel it on the spool. If you fail to do this, even 30-pound-test may dig into the bedding and cause a lost fish.*

Now, don't let me scare you away from using these new braided lines (provided they are of at least 30-pound test), because they do offer two major advantages over the older backing materials.

For example, for small freshwater reels and trout fishing, where the fly line almost fills the spool, these thin diameters offer help. They will permit you to easily add 20 yards or so of backing, which is usually sufficient for most trout situations. Or for the saltwater fly fisherman, if he will *carefully* install the backing properly on the spool, he can add about 50 percent more backing than Dacron or Micron will provide. This increased backing capacity allows the bonefish angler who prefers the smaller saltwater reels to fish with adequate backing. Or, for the angler who is seeking long-running fish, such as billfish, it allows him to put considerably more yards of line on his reel than Dacron or Micron can provide. Moreover, such thin lines have considerably less resistance against the water when the fish makes a long run.

It is worth noting here that when backing is the cause of a lost fish, in the majority of cases the loss was not caused by type of line being used, but rather the improper installation of the backing. This is true of any type of backing you use. So, regardless of whether you are using Dacron, Micron, squidding line, or one of the new braided lines, keep in mind that it is extremely important that the backing be placed on the spool under pressure, so that the bedding is *firm and overlapping line cannot dig into it.*

Regarding backing line strength and weight, the two sizes used most often today are 20 or 30-pound test. There are two important factors you should consider in determining which test strength should be used: 1) how large is the reel spool — if it's too small you won't be able to get very much 30-pound-test line on it; 2) how strong is the leader tippet — you obviously don't want to use backing that has less strength than the tippet you are fishing, because if the backing breaks, you can lose everything — leader, fly line, fly, and fish.

Many fly fishermen who seek sea trout, bonefish, redfish, and other species which don't require a heavy leader tippet and where light and comfortable small reels can be used will often select 20-pound-test Dacron or Micron. However, I prefer to use 30-pound-test Dacron or Micron for almost all my backing needs on fly reels.

If you want to conduct an enlightening test, take a two-foot strand of 20-pound-test Dacron or Micron and another strand of the same material with the strength of 30-pound test. Have someone hold a fly rod firmly in front of you. Insert the end of one of the strands in the butt or stripping guide. Grasp the two ends and saw the line rapidly back and forth about 30 or 40 times. Then, repeat this, using the other strand. Now, compare both pieces (you may need a magnifying glass). It may surprise you that the 20-pound-test line will likely resemble a barbed wire fence, though the 30-pound-test line remains intact. Dacron and Micron do abrade. So, if you prefer to use 20-pound-test line, you should make it a practice to check the line fairly often for signs of wear. But 30-pound-test line will last for years.

Another fault many long-time fly fishermen make is to never replace backing. It can wear out. Abusive conditions can ruin even new backing. For example, if you are fishing a coral-studded flat and a fish makes a long run, the line will be dragged over the sharp rocks, creating the distinct possibility that the backing can be nicked or frayed.

Of course, the reason that we use backing in our fly line rigging is that it provides enough line length for us to stay attached to an escaping fish, no matter how far it runs. But let me assure you, outdoor writers and fly fishermen have for years vastly over-rated the distance that most fish run. Blue-fish and stripers will *rarely* run farther than 125 yards of backing (plus 30 yards of fly line). I've caught some large stripers and bluefish on the fly — even up to 18 pounds — and none ever took out more than 100 yards of backing plus fly line.

Or bonefish. They are legendary for supposed runs of 250 yards. Now, I am not sure how many bonefish I have caught over 10 pounds, but it has been quite a few. *And I must say, in my experience, no bonefish I've ever hooked has run more than a fly line and 150 yards of backing.* Think about it: if you included the fly line and leader, that is nearly two football fields away! Moreover, many fly fishermen who seek snook, redfish, sea trout and similar species routinely carry reels loaded with 250 to 300 yards of backing. This amount of backing will *never* be needed.

Of course, there are some fishing situations where a lot of backing is demanded. You'll need a lot of line (at least 300 to 400 yards) for billfish and some of the other offshore speed-sters exceeding 40 pounds in weight, such as wahoo, tuna, and mackerel. And giant tarpon have been known to pull a lot of backing from a reel, especially if the angler is fighting from a staked or anchored boat. *But with these few exceptions, a fly fisherman who has a reel loaded with his fly line plus 150 yards of backing will almost never in his lifetime ever hook a fish that will run beyond the distance of his rigging.*

SOME BACKING TRICKS

Here are several tricks regarding backing that you may want to consider.

1) Some anglers use fly line and backing that are identical or closely similar in color. That is not a good idea! I prefer to connect a backing that is markedly different in color from my fly line so that I have a clear indication when the fish is into my backing on its run. This is important knowledge to possess in a number of fly-fishing situations: in saltwater, for example, when I am near surface obstructions — a stake or a channel buoy or another skiff — whose distance from me I can roughly estimate — and the fish is headed toward one of those obstructions upon which it may wrap itself and break my line. In this situation, the color-coded lengths of my fly line and backing give me a measuring tool for locating the distance and course of the fish, so that I can change my fighting tactics to turn it in another direction. Or in freshwater — particularly in canyons with large boulders — I want to know

when I need to start moving upstream or downstream, over or under the boulders, or to perform any other acrobatics I am capable of, to turn that fish and prevent a break-off.

Since backing comes in many colors, ranging from fluorescent colors to dull reddish-brown, some anglers will use various lengths of different colored backing to tip them off in situations like these. For example, you can connect 100 feet of bright chartreuse backing to the fly line; to that could be connected 100 feet of a different color, etc.

To connect backing lines in this manner, I recommend you use loops. For example, Bimini Twists can be made in both ends of each color of backing so that they can be looped together. If you haven't yet learned how to tie these connections, have your local fly shop build blind spliced loops in all your backing lines for you.

2) There is one other way of modifying the backing that is a real asset, I believe, when you are fighting billfish; and many experienced tarpon fishermen feel it helps them subdue fish they may not have taken otherwise. Billfish and tarpon — or any fish that jumps with great frequency and ferocity — can lunge against the leader and break it. Now, I know there are some fly fishermen who fish a great deal for such species who will scorn any effort to change their rigging to reduce the shock of a large leaping fish against their leader. But, for those of you who only occasionally encounter these jumpers, there is a way of building a shock absorber into the backing that will reduce the chances of a leaping fish breaking your leader or ripping your fly loose.

Connect 100 feet of 25 or 30-pound brightly colored nylon monofilament with a Bimini Twist Loop *to the rear of the fly line*. Then connect the other end of the nylon monofilament to your backing with a loop-to-loop system. You now have backing on the reel, in front of it the 100 feet of bright mono and finally, the fly line. When a fish jumps, if you have the fly line and the monofilament outside the rod tip, the mono will stretch like a giant rubber band. This aids in preventing the leader from snapping. You want brightly colored monofilament, so that your boat operator can see it during the battle and doesn't run over it — which has happened to me.

3) While modern saltwater fly reels require little maintenance, most saltwater fly fishermen make it a practice to wash their reels in freshwater after a day on the salt. But few pay attention to the condition of their backing. They should. Because if during the day they fought a fish that took out a good deal of their backing, it will have soaked up a lot of saltwater and become encrusted with salt, which is a corrosive.

I recommend that at the end of your fishing day or your trip, you fill a sink with *warm soapy water* and place the backing in it. Wash the spool sides with the same soapy water and

How to Use an Arbor Knot or a Uni-Knot (Duncan Loop) to Connect Backing to the Fly Reel Spool

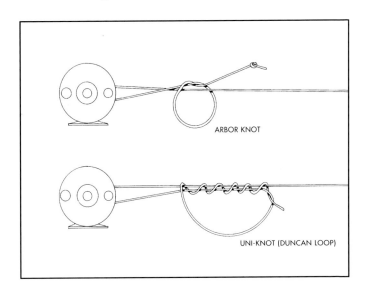

ARBOR KNOT

UNI-KNOT (DUNCAN LOOP)

wipe clean. Drain the soapy water, flush the backing line with clear water, and replace it firmly on the spool.

Backing is often ignored when fly tackle is considered, but it forms a vital link between you and a trophy fish and deserves your attention.

You need to securely connect the backing to the reel spool axle. There are two popular knots that accomplish this. The Uni-Knot (also called the Duncan Loop) is a good one for this purpose. Another option is the Arbor Knot, which is not as strong, but rarely fails.

Now that the backing has been securely fastened to the spool axle, and the backing is *firmly* wound up on the spool, we can turn to the fly line connection.

OVERLEAF: *Two fishing companions enjoying an Atlantic salmon stream in Iceland.*

CHAPTER THREE

FLY LINE CONNECTIONS

CONNECTING BACKING TO FLY LINE

Let's begin by examining the criteria for a proper backing/fly line connection. First, as I've stated before, but it bears repeating: *any connection should be as strong as the backing,* or very close to its strength. Second, it must pass smoothly through the rod guides and tip *going out and returning.* Some knots pass smoothly through the rod guides when traveling in one direction, but not in the other. Two good examples of such connections are the Albright Knot and the Nail Knot.

With the Albright, the fly line is folded over (in a horse-shoe shape) to connect the backing to it. One leg of the Albright is therefore the stub of the fly line. Unless this stub is coated with something to create a smooth joint, it can catch on a guide or tip top as the fish pulls the knot through.

Similarly, the Nail Knot has a stub, and unless a smooth coating is placed over it on the return of the line to the reel, the stub can catch in the guides.

And, while it's not a criterion, I think you'll find it's a definite plus if the connection is quick and easy to disconnect when you want to exchange one line for another.

As I mentioned when I was discussing how to construct one earlier in the book, my personal choice for connecting the backing loop to the fly line is the Whipped Loop. When properly constructed, this loop is stronger than the fly line. And because it is a rounded and smooth connection, with no protruding ends, it is able to pass smoothly in and out of the guides, free of trouble. Also, it has the quick-change advantages that a loop provides. I urge you to try the Whipped Loop. Review its construction (discussed and illustrated on pages 19-23). With a minimal amount of practice you will find you can make one in less than two minutes!

Another connection favored by some experienced anglers is the Double Nail Knot Loop (illustrated on pages 75-77). But there remains the chance that a small protruding stub may be formed when this knot is finished. However, a smooth joint can be made (and incidentally, this can also be done with the Albright and Nail knots) by coating the knot with Goop, Pliobond, Aqua-Seal, or a similar flexible glue. Use enough to form a taper resembling the shape of a football on both sides of the knot.

Commercial braided leader loops can be used to connect the backing to the fly line, too. Packets of these loops, which you can purchase at fly shops, generally provide joining instructions. The technique is fast and simple.

There are a number of other methods of connecting fly lines to backing, but any one of the options mentioned here should be sufficient for your needs.

CONNECTING THE FLY LINE TO THE LEADER

I will discuss later how to make various connections within a fly line to allow you to connect shooting heads to heavier front portions, or join two different fly lines, etc. But first, as illustrated on the opposite page, this section focuses on the several ways the angler can attach a leader to the fly line.

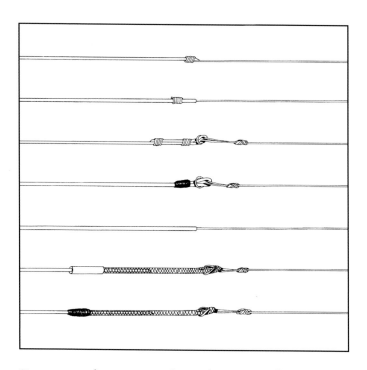

From top to bottom — *Tube Nail Knot, Needle Nail Knot, Double Nail Knot Loop, Whipped Loop, Glued Joint, commercial Braided Leader Loop, and homemade Braided Whipped Loop.*

While there are a number of methods of attaching the leader to the fly line, there is only one way that I caution you *not to use*, and that is the small *metal eye splice*, a commercial device resembling a short needle, barbed along the shank, and ending in a tiny, ringed eye. The connection is made by inserting the sharp end of the device into the fly line until only the eye is visible. The leader is attached to the eye. The small barbs embedded into the fly line are supposed to hold the gadget in place. But it just doesn't work as advertised. This is a most unsatisfactory way to connect a leader to the fly line.

Tube Nail Knot

This is perhaps the most commonly used connection to attach a leader to a fly line. It has the advantage of being easy to do. When properly made, it is a strong connection. It also flows well through the guides if it is correctly trimmed and the joint smoothed with glue.

Joe Brooks, famed outdoor writer of the 1950s and 1960s, discovered this knot when fishing in Argentina. Natives there used a tapered horseshoe nail to make the knot — hence the name "Nail Knot". Joe wrote about the knot in *Outdoor Life* and it was truly a revelation when compared to the various other crude knots being used at the time. However, many people encountered tying problems when using the nail. Then someone came up with the idea of using a tube instead.

You can see from the illustration just how the knot is tied. The neat thing about tying this knot with a tube, rather than the horseshoe nail, is that it reduces the diameter of the coils formed when making the knot. Because after the nail or tube has been extracted, these coils need to be closed firmly. Over time, it was found that the smaller the tube, the less trouble was encountered when drawing the coils tight.

The Tube Nail Knot is an excellent knot to learn. Its principal use today is to attach the leader butt to the fly line, but there are other methods of using this important connection that I'll be discussing later.

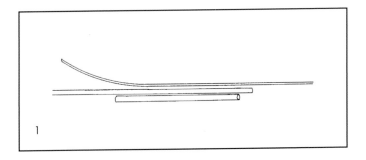

1

Step 1) Lay a small tube alongside the end of the fly line. Then take the butt section of the leader and place about 4 inches of the tag end toward the back end of the fly line.

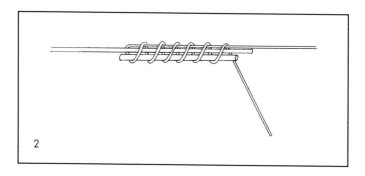

Step 2) Grip the leader butt, fly line, and needle firmly and make a series of three to seven wraps over all three pieces toward the end of the fly line as shown. *Note:* for the purpose of the illustration the wraps are shown slightly separated, but the closer the wraps are made to each other, the easier it will be to make the final closure of the knot.

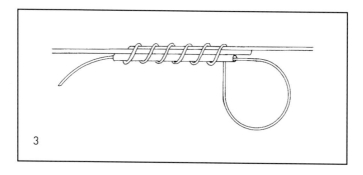

Step 3) Insert the leader butt end in one end of the tube and push out the other end. *Always hold the wraps during all tying steps or they will unravel.*

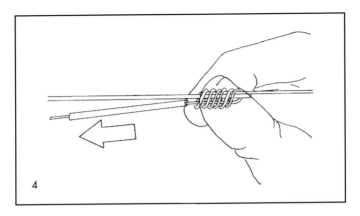

Step 4) Now, remove the tube by sliding it from under the wraps and lay it aside.

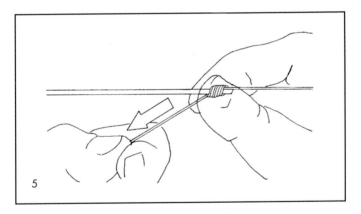

Step 5) Always pull on the tag end first to close the knot. If you pull on the main leader, the wraps will slip off the fly line. Once the knot is closed firmly by pulling with the tag end, grasp the tag end and the main leader and pull them both as tight as possible.

Step 6) Clip the tag end as close to the knot as possible. Some people will now form a small football-shaped joint over the

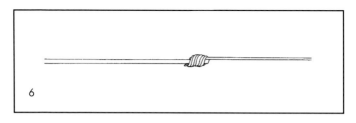

6

knot with a glue, such as Pliobond or Goop. This allows the Nail Knot to slip easily through the guides.

Important: There are a few special fly lines that a Nail Knot will not work with. One example is Scientific Anglers' Monocore fly line. Because this line has a nylon core with a coating of clear nylon, under stress any type of Nail Knot will just slip off the line. Should you be using this type of line, I suggest that you use one of the loop knots for a better connection. I have already mentioned several (the Whipped Loop, Surgeon's Loop, Non-Slip Mono Loop), any of which will work on such specialty lines. If you do decide to use a Nail Knot, always test it before fishing it on any line.

Double Nail Knot Loop

This knot has already been addressed in the discussion on how to attach backing to the fly line. It can be used for the same purpose to attach the leader to the fly line. Be sure to test the loop for strength before fishing it.

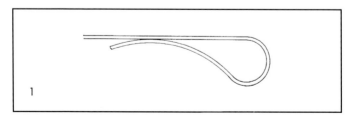

1

Step 1) Fold the fly line end back about 2 inches.

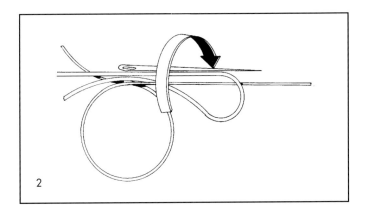

Step 2) Make a Speedy Nail Knot (see pages 24-27 for instructions and illustrations for this knot).

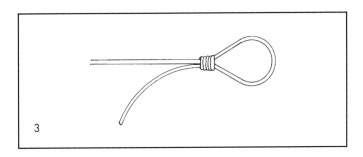

Step 3) Close the knot securely and be sure to trim the tag ends flush against the knot.

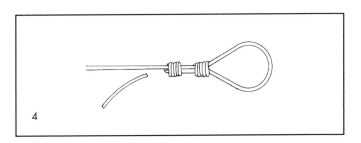

Step 4) Make another Speedy Nail Knot and close it firmly. Trim the tag ends flush against the knot and cut the fly line end so that it tapers and lies tightly against the first Nail Knot that you tied.

Needle Nail Knot

If you are going to use a Nail Knot, this one makes the smoothest and strongest connection. The illustrations demonstrate how the knot is made. The butt section of the leader is inserted into the center of the line end, pulled out back a little way, and the coils encircle the line. This leaves a connection that slips in and out of the guides and never snags in the guides.

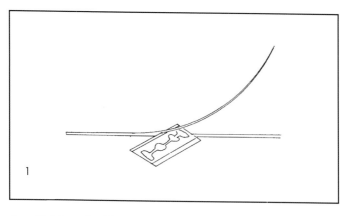

Step 1) Use a double-edged razor blade (a single-edged blade rarely is sharp enough). Begin about 2 inches from the end of your leader butt, slicing the monofilament with the razor blade. (This may seem difficult, but it is really quite easy.) Make several slices, each one closer to the end than the last one. This will create a taper in the leader end. When you have shaved the end of the leader down to a thickness as fine as a hair, you are ready for the next step.

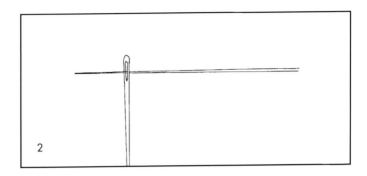

Step 2) Insert the tapered end of the leader in a *small* needle (this won't work with a larger needle).

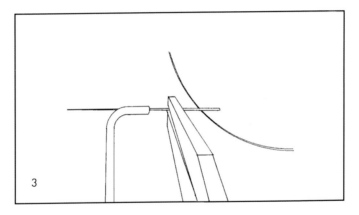

Step 3) Using a pair of pliers or hemostats, grasp the needle firmly and work the end into the center of your fly line. Force the needle back through the center at least 5/16 of an inch and then out the side of the fly line. Be careful not to lose the leader that is held in the needle eye.

Step 4) Firmly grip the fly line end with the thumb and first finger. Grasp the pointed end of the needle with the pliers and pull the needle and the tapered end of the leader through the fly line.

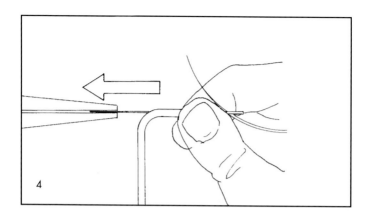

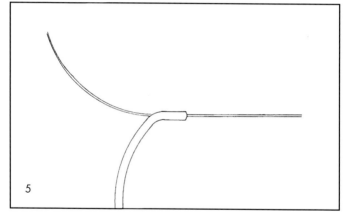

Step 5) Bring about 4 inches of the leader through the line and out of the exit point.

Step 6) Using a *larger* needle, with a fairly open eye, lay the needle against the fly line with the eye at the forward end of the line. Make three or four wraps over the fly line, where the leader comes out of the exit point. Be particularly careful to grip these wraps firmly as they are made so they don't unravel. While gripping the wraps, slip the tapered end of the mono-filament through the needle eye.

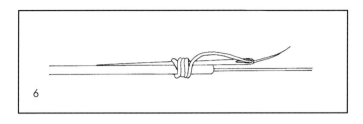

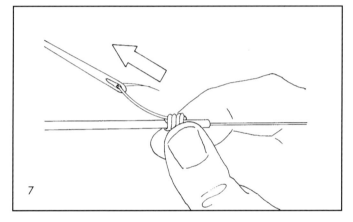

Step 7) While holding the wraps firmly together, use a pair of pliers to pull the needle and the end of the monofilament underneath the wraps.

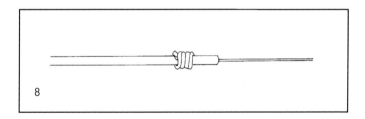

Step 8) Firmly close the knot so that the leader buries down into the fly line coating. Then, clip the tag end of the leader flush with the wraps.

Braided Leader Loop

This is a commercially manufactured loop consisting of hollow, braided leader material. Generally, a simple shrink tube device is supplied with the commercial loop.

The illustrations show how to connect a commercial Braided Leader Loop to a fly line. Using a straight piece of braided leader material, this same technique can be used to connect one fly line to another. When connecting two different fly line lengths (such as when constructing a shooting head), don't use the shrink tubing. Instead, to prevent the braided ends from fraying, make a Whipped Loop at the very ends of the braided material. Or, to secure the ends so they don't fray, make a Nail Knot using 8 or 10-pound-test mono.

How to Connect a Commercial Loop to the Fly Line

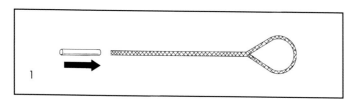

Step 1) Cut off approximately 3/8 of an inch of the shrink tubing (which is supplied with the commercial Braided Leader Loop package). Slide it over the end of the braid and gently push it up until it snugs against the loop.

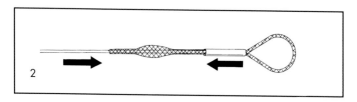

Step 2) Carefully slide the end of the fly line into the tubing.

By teasing the braided portion, you can gradually work the fly line end up until it is against the loop.

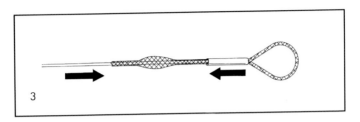

Step 3) If you have frayed the ends quite a bit, trim the loose strands with scissors. Now, slide the shrink tubing forward until a part of it has passed the frayed ends and encircles the fly line. If you now heat the tubing it will shrink and hold the frayed ends securely. *Don't overheat,* since this could ruin the braid and the fly line. A good way to shrink the tubing is simply to hold it near a bare light bulb.

CONNECTIONS TO MODIFY FLY LINES

Fly fishermen often need to modify their fly lines to suit existing fishing conditions, perhaps by adding some element to the fly line, or to connect two or more kinds of lines together to make one. But if you fish with sinking lines, there is an important line modification that I recommend you learn and use — the Tube Nail Knot Trick.

The Tube Nail Knot Trick

Imagine this situation. I am watching an angler using a weight-forward slow-sinking monofilament fly line — called a "slime line" by some tarpon anglers. Three times he threw

Fishing on Quitta Creek, Pennsylvania.➤

at big tarpon. Two of the casts were flawed and each time another cast had to be made. One presentation was perfect, at least we thought so. But the tarpon ignored the offering and another cast was required. In every instance, it was the second cast that got the fisherman in trouble. Because on each of his fishing opportunities, the tarpon was moving and the second throw had to be made quickly. We all know that a hurried cast is almost always a poor one.

Another time I watched a companion working a reef in 40 feet of water just east of the Turneffe Islands in Belize. He was using a Uniform Sink Line, designed so that the forward end of the line sinks as fast as does the belly section — something that has been a problem with most sinking lines for decades. *This line is the same color throughout its length.* The angler would cast the fly as far as he could (the length of the line) and allow it to sink deep. Then he would start his retrieve. If no strike was forthcoming, he would make a back cast and repeat the routine. My friend was working so hard at casting that he began to sweat and finally sat down disgusted with the whole procedure.

Another time I was fishing for stripers in New England with a friend who was using a weight-forward sinking line. It was dark green in color throughout its length. A cast was made and a retrieve completed. Then the angler would attempt to roll the sinking line out of the water and make another forward cast. Again, the problem was lifting the correct amount of line from the water to execute a roll pick-up cast.

When using any sinking line, the real problem for the fly fisherman is how much line should be retrieved before an attempt is made to lift the line and roll all of it out of the water prior to making the back cast. Because actually, once a sinking line is out of the water, casting it is pretty easy. But, it is the act of getting the line above the surface prior to making the back cast that creates the most problems for many fly fishermen.

If you strip in too much line, e.g., more line than is actually required for an effective cast, you will have to make additional false casts to extend a sufficient amount of line outside the rod tip to load the rod for a decent forward cast. Or, if you try to pick up too much line, e.g., more line than you are actually capable of lifting above the surface of the water, you will fail since when you attempt to make a roll cast pick-up, the portion of the line still underwater will pull against the amount of line you have cleared and cause it to collapse in a mess in front of you, forcing you to start all over again.

What has created these types of problems is that many of the sinking fly lines today are of a uniform color. Or, in the case of the slime line, the entire line is clear. So, as the fly fisherman retrieves line there is no reference point to indicate to him when the correct amount of line — neither too little nor too much — is outside his rod tip, the amount of line that will permit him to execute a proper and easy roll pick-up cast. Of course, this presents a problem to line manufacturers, because there is no one length standard to apply. Obviously, the strength and skill level of casters differs. For example, a good caster will be able to lift and roll cast more sinking line from underneath the water than one possessing lesser skills.

But, fortunately, there is a very simple solution to this problem that will work for everybody, at every skill level, and one that is really very easy to do.

Take a sinking line rig to the edge of the water and make a number of casts. Each time the line is retrieved, note the length of line you have lifted from underneath the water, and exactly what amount of line you need to lift in order to execute a good roll pick-up cast. When you are pretty sure of the length of line that you can handle well, extend that exact amount of line beyond your rod tip, and with a permanent pen place a mark on the fly line at a spot just opposite your stripping hand. At this point you will have found your solution to the prob-

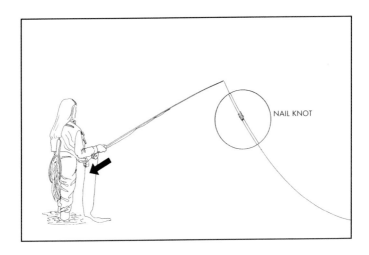

Mid-Line Tube Nail Knot

lem and you could go no further, just retrieving and casting your sinking line properly by relying on that mark. But marks can over time be erased by the effects of water and sun on the ink and are hard to see under even the best light conditions. And even more importantly, to rely on the mark, you will have to look at and concentrate on the line in your stripping hand during the retrieve, a critical time when your attention should be focused on fishing and the fish.

So let's take the idea one step further. Bring the line home and locate the mark you made. Using 10 or 12-pound-test monofilament, install a conventional Tube Nail Knot on the line at the place where you made the mark. Be sure to really tighten on both ends of the knot to bury most of the turns of monofilament into the fly line coating. Then, trim the ends cleanly. Note that you want to do this with a Tube Nail Knot (see tying instructions on pages 72-75), as you can't tie the Speedy Nail Knot or the Needle Nail Knot in the middle of a fly line. Now, go to the water, make a cast and begin a retrieve.

You won't have to look at the line, just concentrate on fishing. Although the monofilament Tube Nail Knot is very tiny and almost buried in the fly line coating, as it rides across your stripping finger you will easily feel it. When you do, immediately stop your retrieve, make a roll pick-up cast, and you will suddenly delight in using sinking lines.

This same Tube Nail Knot trick may also save you fish, especially when trying for bonefish, tarpon, redfish, or permit. With these saltwater species, the usual fly-fishing procedure is to stand on the casting platform of a skiff and strip off enough line so that you can make whatever quick cast is needed. In this situation, the problem that so many fly fishermen have is that they strip off *too much line*, so that they have excess line lying all over the deck which is liable to become tangled in shoe strings, rod holders, tackle boxes, or what have you.

An experienced saltwater fly fisherman will instead strip off only the amount of line actually needed for casting, keeping the rest of his fly line safely stored on the reel. For most anglers 50 feet of line lying on the deck is about all that's needed for normal fly-fishing situations in shallow water. So, with 50 feet (or whatever length you desire) of line extended outside the rod tip, install a Tube Nail Knot in your fly line at the spot just opposite your stripping hand. You'll have a fixed and certain casting distance marker available to you from then on.

OVERLEAF: *Fly fishing for trout in the western United States.*

CHAPTER FOUR

SHOOTING HEADS

A WORD ABOUT SHOOTING HEADS

For most anglers, the toughest challenge in fly fishing is being able to cast a long line to reach distant targets or to swim the fly through a considerable amount of water. We all recognize, I think, that the ability to make longer casts, or accomplish an extended retrieve, can make a considerable difference in whether or not we score.

Coupled with the distance problem is that fly fishermen are confronted by the wind nearly all the time. There are many fishing situations in which God will not allow us to cast downwind. More often than not we have to throw into it. This is especially true for those who fish in saltwater. Surf fishermen are always confronted with a breeze blowing in their face.

Another difficulty that fly fishermen often struggle with is getting their fly deep enough in the water column. In many situations being able to swim the fly just a few feet deeper can mean more hook-ups.

Conventional weight-forward lines are fine for casting to 60 or so feet. But there are important occasions when repetitive casting at more than 70 feet is called for. Using conventional weight-forward lines, it takes a strong and experienced fly fisherman to keep casting that far for any length of time. And the problem is aggravated when using a sinking line, as sinking weight-forward lines have a rear section that is rather large in diameter, which serves to reduce the ability to shoot the fly to the desired target, and also impedes the descent of the sinking line.

To a large measure, these distance, wind, and water depth problems can be solved by replacing your conventional fly line with a shooting head/shooting line rig. If you are not currently using a shooting head/line rig for long distance or great depth fishing situations, I suggest you try it. You may like it.

The shooting head/shooting line rig came into being many years ago, when tournament casters came to realize that by attaching extra-thin line behind the heavy forward portion of a fly line they could obtain greater distance. Such a heavy front portion of a fly line section is now commonly called a "shooting head" by most anglers (which is the term by which I will refer to it, bowing to common practice), although the correct designation is "shooting taper." The commercial product is designated as "ST." Thus, a commercial shooting taper matched to an 8-weight rod would be labeled ST8F (Shooting Taper size 8 Floating).

Many anglers simply purchase commercial shooting heads, which are generally manufactured in a length of 30 feet, in designated line weights to match their designated rod weights. But that's not a practice I recommend. First of all, just 30 feet of line extended beyond the rod tip is not a good length for long distance casting. (When casting with a conventional weight-forward fly line, most fly fishermen are actually accustomed to extending more than 30 feet of line outside their rod tip for longer casts.) In response to their dissatisfaction with the commercial 30-foot shooting head, these days more and more anglers are beginning to make their own shooting heads at various longer lengths. Moreover — and this is critically important — *for distance casting, using a shooting head one designated line size larger than your designated rod size is recommended, because the increased weight permits you to shoot line over a longer distance.* It's quite easy to do, so you should buy a double taper line *one size larger than the rod calls for.* For example, if you are using a 9-weight rod, buy a 10-weight double taper. You can make two shooting heads from this double taper line, since the mid-section of a double taper line is level, tapering exactly the same way at each end.

Depending upon how good a caster you are, measure back from one end beyond 30 feet and cut the line. If you are a good caster (let's define that as an angler who can easily throw 70 feet with a weight-forward line) then cut off 38 feet of the line. This means you will have a shooting head 8 feet longer than a commercial 30-footer. This will unroll a longer distance toward the target before it begins falling. Of course, if you later determine that 38 feet is too much length for you to handle, you can simply shorten it.

After you have purchased a commercial shooting head, you will need to attach it to a thinner line, called a "shooting line." Line manufacturers sell both shooting heads and shooting lines. Commercial shooting lines are simply level lines.

For saltwater fly fishing you need to know that commercial shooting lines with a diameter less than .030 may test less than 15 pounds. To be safe, use a shooting line that measures .035 or slightly larger, since smaller diameter shooting lines are often weaker than the leader tippet. During a fish-fight, if enough strain is put on tackle equipped with a shooting line of .030 or smaller, the shooting line, instead of the leader, may break, losing the shooting head and the fish.

Fly fishermen use a number of materials for shooting lines, ranging from monofilament (usually 25 to 40 pounds in test) to braided leader butt material, as well as a variety of commercial shooting lines.

If you want to obtain the most distance, and obtain the greatest depth with a shooting head, then a shooting line of monofilament is supreme. Many people, however, feel that this light material blows around too much in a breeze, and tends to tangle.

Braided leader butt line material is okay, too, and it shoots exceptionally well. But it is very rough on the hands, and with repeated use it can really cut through the skin. Of course, taping over your fingers can eliminate much of this problem.

CONNECTING SHOOTING HEADS
AND SHOOTING LINES

Once you have purchased or constructed a shooting head, you will need to connect it to the shooting line. There are several methods of doing this connection. You can put a Whipped Loop in both the shooting head and the shooting line, and then simply join the two lines by looping one to the other (see the illustrations on how to make a Whipped Loop and making the loop-to-loop connection on pages 19-23). Be sure to try to make your loops no larger than about 1/4 inch, as the smaller the connected loops, the easier they will slip through the rod guides when retrieving line.

The special advantage of the loop-to-loop connection is that it gives you the ability at streamside to quickly exchange your existing shooting head for another as fishing situations change. The disadvantage of this connection is that loops do tend to run roughly through the rod guides. However, making the Whipped Loops as small as possible can reduce much of this problem.

Another way to connect a shooting head to a shooting line is with braided leader butt material. Cut off about 5 inches of braided butt leader material. Then tease open one end of this material with a large needle. Insert the shooting line half-

Casting to stripers on Martha's Vineyard. ➤

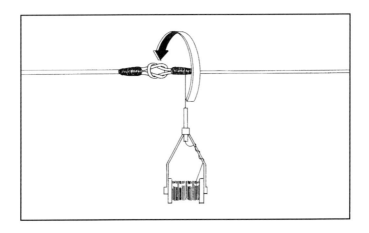

How to Connect a Shooting Head to a Shooting Line with a Whipped Loop

way through the inside of the braid to a depth of about 1 1/2 inches. You may have to tease it a little to get it inside. Then, with a razor blade, cut an angle on the back of the shooting head. By working carefully you can then tease the tapered end of the shooting head well back into the braided material until it butts up against the shooting line inside the braid. Finish off the job by securing the fuzzy ends of the braided material. There are three ways to do this: you can trim the fuzz, and then whip finish the ends; or tie a Tube Nail Knot to secure the ends; or simply glue both fraying ends of the braided material to prevent it from unraveling further. What is important *is to secure only the ends of the braided material. Allow the rest of the shooting head and line to nestle relaxed inside the braided line.* Under tension, the braided line will act like a Chinese finger and clench the shooting head and line so tightly that you can't pull them apart. This makes a really smooth loop connection that will flow in and out of the guides, much like a conventional weight-forward line.

How to Connect a Shooting Head to a Shooting Line with Braided Leader Material

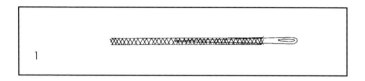

1

Step 1) Cut a 5-inch length of 30 or 50-pound braided leader material line (as far as I know, only Cortland Line Company manufactures braided leader material in the 50-pound strength) and insert a large needle into it (to relax the braid).

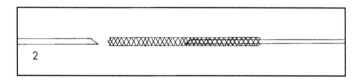

2

Step 2) Insert the shooting line halfway through the inside of the braid. Cut the rear end of the shooting head (which will be larger in diameter) to a taper and push it into the braid until it butts against the end of the line.

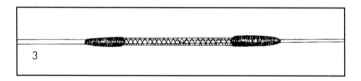

3

Step 3) Trim loose strands and make a Whipped Loop on both ends of the braided material. *Be sure to whip no more than 1/4 inch of the braided ends. The rest of the braid must be untouched.* The braid acts like a Chinese finger: the harder you pull on the lines, the more securely the braid grips the line inside it. Coat the ends with glue.

Commercial shooting heads are generally made in only one material throughout their length, i.e., lead core, floating, various sinking rate densities, sink tip, etc. But, you may want to combine several types of line within a single shooting head. For example, you may want to use a floating head, but have the last several feet sink rapidly. By building a loop in the forward end of the head, and then looping on either a short length of lead-core or fast-sinking line, you can obtain the desired results. Or, for deep-water conditions, Dan Blanton showed me a unique head he has devised. He chops off the first 10 feet of a commercial fast-sinking head, and builds a loop. Then, depending upon how deep he wants to fish his fly, he will loop on lengths of lead-core line that vary from 5 to 10 feet in length. Using various combinations of lead core, I find this line to be one of the most versatile of all shooting heads. And it's easy to cast with a water haul.

Another modification I like to use is one I call the "sailfish or leaping fish line." A fish struggling underwater against the angler is encumbered by the water it is swimming against, and is restricted from exerting great pressure or making jolting jerks against either the fragile tippet or the hook that is barely biting into its flesh. But once that fish leaps above the surface, factors change. Now, the fish can throw its full weight violently against the leader and line. *In this situation, the key to preventing a tippet breaking or hook pulling free is to have controlled slack in the line while the fish is airborne.* As I have mentioned many times in the Library, the two techniques used over the years to combat this problem involve either bowing or dipping the rod toward the fish. These two techniques require that the angler feed slack while the fish is in the air, preventing the fish from gaining full leverage against the hook or leader tippet.

Bowing and dipping work well when battling large tarpon, if you have some experience at the game. But the factors change when you hook a fast running billfish. Generally, when a billfish feels the steel of a hook, it makes a long and frantic run. Such runs can easily be 150 yards or more. Bowing or dipping doesn't work here for good reason. Many times the sailfish is so far away when it leaps that it is in the air and back in the water before the angler can bow or dip the rod. Thus, the fish is using its full strength against the line and leader before slack can be given.

There is a modification to a fly line used for billfish that will solve this critical problem. *This same modified line works very well for tarpon and other leaping saltwater fish.* Some experienced guides and anglers look down their nose at the idea. They feel that it is unnecessary. In truth, they don't need it because they know when and how to bow or dip. But, if you have little experience at battling giant tarpon, billfish, or other species that make many leaps at some distance from the boat, this modified line just might help you land a trophy.

Here is how the fly line — all types of line: floating, slow sinking, fast sinking or lead core — is modified. Cut the line at about 40 feet from the front end. Make a loop of your choice in the forward section where you made the cut. Discard the rear of the fly line (you will be using only the 40 feet for casting). Then, measure 100 feet of 25 or 30-pound brightly colored monofilament. The mono can be any standard line used for casting or trolling. But, it must be brightly colored, preferably, a fluorescent yellow or orange. This line needs to be highly visible, and I'll explain why in a moment.

Make a loop in both ends of the monofilament (the Bimini Twist is best for this) and then connect one monofilament loop to the loop at the rear of the fly line. Use the loop in the other end of the monofilament to connect the line to your backing with a loop-to-loop connection.

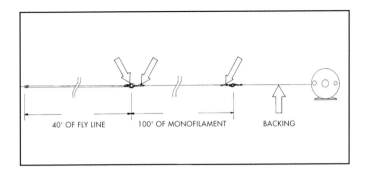

Sailfish Specialty Line Connection

When fishing, this is what happens. The hook is set and the fish takes off. At some distance from the boat the fish leaps. You may be looking directly behind the boat, in the direction where you think the fish is running. But the fish has made an underwater turn and is in the air to your right. There is no time for you to bow toward the fish. It is up and back again before you realize it. No problem, because the 100-foot length of monofilament has stretched so much that there is no opportunity for the fish to rip and tear against your tackle. I like to compare this 100-foot section to a giant rubber band. Remember I emphasized that the 100 feet of mono should be highly visible? The reason will become obvious as the captain chases a fleeing fish. If you use clear or hard-to-see monofilament, during the chase the boat may run over it. If the monofilament is brightly colored, the captain can see and avoid it. And it often gives the angler a better indication of the direction in which the fish is swimming.

This modified line was developed to help fight distant leaping billfish. But, I would like to stress that if you do not have experience fighting giant tarpon, it may mean the difference between tying on another fly or enjoying the thrill of boating your trophy tarpon.

And here is another useful modification. Back in the 1950s, before sinking-tip lines were developed by the manufacturers, Irv Swope, of Frederick, Maryland, and myself began using a special type of sinking line. I have seen some other experienced fishermen over the years use this same line construction, and in some ways it is more versatile than the conventional sink-tip line. Let me explain by first stating a few fishing problems, and then how to solve them quickly, right on the stream, by modifying the line.

You are fishing a trout stream with a floating line. Dry-fly fishing has been great. But, the hatch ends and there is no more surface activity. Here and there you can see the flash that's reflected from a trout as it rolls to grab a nymph. The water is about 4 feet deep. If you are using a loop in the end of your fly line, you can quickly adjust to each situation. Unloop the leader, and loop on a one-foot section of lead-core trolling line. Now you can swim an unweighted (and more lively) nymph pattern where the trout are nymphing.

A little later, you see fish chasing sculpins in a deeper pool. You still have that floating line, but if you loop on 3 feet of lead-core line you have a super fast-sinking tip that will let you get down to the fish.

Let's take another example, far from a trout stream. You are fishing bonefish on a shallow flat. You decide that you would like to have a few snapper for dinner. A nearby channel has numerous coral heads that are apartment houses for snappers. But, even with a Clouser Minnow you can't get the fly deep enough to interest the snappers. No problem, remove the leader and loop on a 6-foot length of lead-core line. You'll find you can swim your fly down deep into snapper territory.

The ability to loop on various lengths of lead-core trolling line to obtain various sink rates can give you the ability to adjust to many fishing situations while using only a floating line. You will need a loop in the fly line end.

One word of caution. When casting with any length of lead core at the very end of the fly line, you will need to modify your casting stroke. Tight loops won't do it here! You'll get hellish tangles in the line end and leader. Instead, if you throw wider loops on the back and forward casts, you'll find you won't have any problems casting even a very long line.

Lead-core trolling line, which has a thin lead wire core inside nylon braid, can be obtained from most fishing stores that sell offshore tackle. The lines come in a variety of strengths. But in almost all cases, line strength of the lead-core line has nothing to do with its sink rate. The diameter of the lead core is the same; only the strength of the material is different.

If you are a trout fisherman, I would suggest making up three different lengths of lead-core line for use as sinking tips. Here are the lengths I suggest for trout: 6 inches, 1 foot, and 2 1/2 feet. In a given day on the water, this variety of sinking tips will permit you to quickly adapt your technique to a wide variety of fishing situations that you may encounter. For bass, steelhead, or salmon fly fishing, I would suggest the following lengths: 1, 2, and 4 feet. For saltwater fly fishing, my preference would be 4, 6, and 8-foot lengths of lead-core line.

Before making loops in these sinking tip sections, you will need to remove about 2 1/2 inches of the lead core from either end. This is a simple procedure. Cut the desired lengths about 4 or 5 inches longer than you feel you need. Grasp the line about an inch from the end with a thumb and forefinger. Push back on the braid at the end to expose the lead core. Grasp the lead and slide the braid back until about 2 or 2 1/2 inches of lead are exposed. Clip off the lead and you can push the braid back into its original position.

There are several ways you can make loops in the ends of these lead-core sections. One very simple way is to fold the coreless braid back and make a loop by tying a simple Overhand Knot. This may look like it won't hold; but, if you pull the knot up tightly, it will never loosen. Trim the standing end snug against the Overhand Knot. Or, you can use a piece of thin wire fashioned into a narrow loop. Insert it into the braided material and pull the line through, as you would do in constructing a braided loop. This makes a very neat connection, and if made properly, will never pull out. Or, you can fold the hollow braid back and make a Double Nail Knot Loop. My favorite way, which takes less than two minutes to do, is to fold the hollow braided portion of the line back onto itself and make a Whipped Loop.

OVERLEAF: *Casting for trout in the Wind River Range, Wyoming.*

CHAPTER FIVE

CONNECTIONS TO MODIFY LEADERS

The basic tapered leader is okay in many fishing situations. But, there are a host of places where you need to slightly modify or make an entirely different type of leader. What follows are some suggestions for making several types of leaders to meet a wide range of fishing situations — basic tapered leaders, leaders composed of a wide variety of monofilament sections, or leaders with braided or solid trolling wire attached.

Three knots are generally used to connect different diameters of monofilament together to make a tapered leader: the Surgeon's Knot, the Blood Knot, and the Simple Blood Knot (see tying instructions for the latter two knots on page 159 of a companion volume in the Library, *American Masters Fly Fishing Symposium: Volume Two — Tackle*).

THE BASIC TAPERED LEADER

With the exception of dry-fly presentations, the basic leader formula that follows on the next page will permit you to make good tapered leaders for almost any fly-fishing situation in which a tapered design is required.

Before listing the formula, I would like to caution that, whenever possible, all sections of a tapered leader should be made from the same type of monofilament. In my opinion, the use of hard or stiff mono for the butt section inhibits good casting, so don't use this material in the butt. And, my experience shows that when making your leaders, you'll get the best results by combining varying strengths of monofilament manufactured by the same company primarily for use on spinning reels (such manufacturers as DuPont, Maxima, Berkeley, Silver Queen, etc.).

Now the formula. Cut a length of monofilament for a butt section. The next, or second, smaller section should be half the length of the butt section. The next, or third, smaller section should be half the length of the second. The last, or fourth, section should be half the length of the third section. Then, add about 2 feet of tippet. *Important:* you don't have to be exact in your measurements. If you are a few inches off it won't matter. This formula has worked well for me for years. Such a tapered leader can be used for steelhead, Atlantic salmon, large and smallmouth bass, trout fishing with nymphs — really in every situation I can think of where a tapered leader is desirable. It can even work pretty well for dry-fly fishing if that's all you have available.

What the formula means is that you will have to first decide how heavy (or of what diameter) a butt section you will need, and then how long you want the butt section to be. This decision will ultimately determine the leader length. Let me give two examples: For one of the best tapered leaders for bass and many other similar fishing conditions, the following leader works well: Cut a 4-foot length of 25-pound monofilament for the butt. Then, add 2 feet of 20-pound mono (half the butt length). Then, secure 1 foot of 15-pound mono, followed by *approximately* 6 inches of 12-pound mono. Add about 2 feet of 10 or 8-pound mono for a tippet. This will

A float trip in Alaska. ➤

give you a 9 1/2-foot leader — one of the most practical lengths for a tapered leader.

Or, let's assume that you are going after bonefish. These fish are very easily frightened, so you'll need a longer leader. I have found that a leader of at least 12 feet is best for such fishing; and if it's calm, a leader even a little longer is desirable. Because there are frequently stiff winds encountered on the flats, I start my bonefish tapered leader with 6 feet of 30-pound mono. I then add to the butt section a 3-foot length of 25-pound mono, and connect to that about 18 inches of 20-pound mono. Then I attach *approximately* 9 inches of 15-pound test, finishing off with a 2-foot tippet of 12 or 10-pound test. This gives me a leader approximately 13 feet in length — ideal for most bonefishing situations.

Using this basic tapered leader formula and a paper and pencil, you can quickly establish how to make any tapered leader for your fishing conditions.

THE DRY-FLY LEADER

The George Harvey Dry-Fly Leader

George Harvey was, to my knowledge, the first person to emphasize the importance of the tippet in dry-fly fishing. That is, if there are no little "S" curves or small sine waves in the tippet immediately in front of the dry fly, drag will occur. Drag causes more refusals by trout than any other factor.

To obtain those cherished natural waves in the tippet, a tapered leader, from butt to fly, must be constructed with the proper proportions. Over decades of fishing, George has perfected a leader that many of the top trout fishermen feel is the ultimate for dry-fly fishing.

George Harvey Dry-Fly Leader Formula➤

(APPROX.) 9 1/2-foot Leader to .007 (4X)

NAIL KNOT | .017 | .015 | .013 | .011 | .009 | .008 | .007
LINE | 10" | 20" | 20" | 20" | 12" | 18" | 22" to 28"
| | | HARD NYLON | | | SOFT NYLON |

(APPROX.) 10 1/2-foot Leader to .006 (5X)

NAIL KNOT | .017 | .015 | .013 | .011 | .009 | .008 | .007 | .006
LINE | 10" | 20" | 20" | 20" | 12" | 12" | 18" | 22" to 30"
| | | HARD NYLON | | | | SOFT NYLON |

The Commercial Dry-Fly Leader

There was a time, not too long ago, when many commercial dry-fly and trout tapered leaders were poor performers. It was a trial-and-error exercise until you found one that worked for you. That is no longer true. Almost any commercial leader you buy today is well-designed and will serve you satisfactorily. Most commercial tapered dry-fly leaders are knotless. There are some fishermen that feel that knotless leaders are superior; others feel just the contrary. If you fish in weed-filled streams where the knots may catch the grass during a fish-fight, then, of course, a knotless leader is best. Whichever leader design you choose, my experience has shown that there is no casting distinction between a well-designed continuous tapered leader and a knotted one.

If you don't want to build your own tapered dry-fly leaders, you can purchase one of your choice. However, after you fish it awhile and have made frequent changes of flies, you will have shortened the tippet section. And, because this important portion of the leader has been used to tie additional knots, you may no longer be able to create those desirable waves in front of the fly. A length of tippet must be added. To do this, normally you simply add a length of tippet material to your leader. But after you have done this several times, you will find that in tying the connection knots for the tippet, you will have also begun to use up a fair length of your remaining tapered leader, so that it may no longer be properly tapered. Realizing this, most anglers then discard that leader, replacing it with a new one.

That is not necessary if you will use this simple knot and connection trick. Keeping in mind that the tippet sections of most commercially manufactured dry-fly leaders are less than 20 inches in length, with a new commercial leader I do the following: measuring back 24 inches from the tippet end, I cut off and discard the original tippet. Then, I tie a Non-Slip

Mono Loop into the remaining leader end. Next, I select several sections of tippet material in a variety of strengths that I want to fish with, and in one end of each of these tippet sections I construct a Non-Slip Mono Loop. At the start of the day, I make a loop-to-loop connection between the commercial tapered leader and one of my new tippet sections. Then, as the day goes on, after I have used up the first tippet section I looped on, I discard it and loop another. In this manner, the original length of my tapered leader is never compromised.

Important: if you tie the Non-Slip Mono Loop according to instructions, making the correct number of turns for diameter used (see these instructions on page 48), the knot will usually test at full strength of the tippet.

Also, keep in mind that your new tippet section should be within two sizes of the end of the commercial tapered leader. For example, if you purchased a leader with a 5X-tippet, after cutting off 14 inches, you should not add a tippet stronger than 4X, or weaker than 6X.

The great advantage of using the loop in the end of your leader is the ability to quickly disconnect a tippet and replace it without ruining the basic leader. One leader should last the best part of a season for the average trout fisherman.

You will have to make a series of casts to determine the proper tippet length for the particular fly you are casting. I cover in great detail how to adjust tippet length on pages 75-82 in a companion volume in the Library, *Fly Fishing for Trout, Volume I,* but some basics bear repeating here.

Remember two results must be obtained with your leader. First, it must accurately present your fly to a specific position on the water; and second, the leader must help you achieve a drag-free drift of your fly. The key to getting a drag-free float is the length and diameter (or strength) of the tippet. The only way you can determine what diameter and what length tippet should be used is to tie on the fly and cast it to see if the

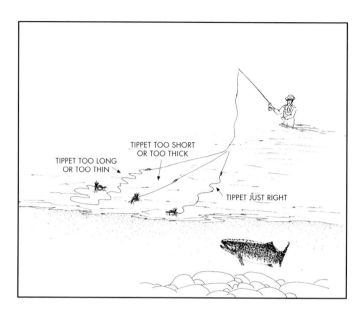

Adjusting Leader Tippets

tippet is okay or needs modifying. I recommend the following procedure: 1) if your cast results in the creation of gentle waves or "S"-shaped curves in the tippet between the fly and the next larger portion of the leader, you have the proper tippet length; 2) but if the tippet falls back on itself or collapses, the tippet is either too long or too thin; or 3) if the tippet falls to the surface in a straight line directly behind the fly, the tippet is either too short or has too large a diameter.

BASIC SALTWATER AND FRESHWATER LEADER WITH BITE TIPPET

There are numerous fly-fishing situations in which the teeth, mouth, or gill cover of the fish we seek will slice through a thin monofilament tippet. In such cases the angler must attach either a special leader of heavy monofilament or wire to prevent a cut-off. This special leader attachment is generally referred to as a "shock tippet." But a better term, I think, is "bite tippet," because there's really no shock phenomenon involved in a cut-off (except maybe the shock to the angler's self-esteem when he loses a big fish!); more commonly it's the anatomy of the fish that creates the problem.

Anglers normally use heavy mono — that is, mono of a pound test that exceeds 30 pounds — to construct their bite tippets, particularly in those fishing situations where the sheen of wire might alert or discourage the fish from striking. Obviously, the strength of the mono must match the fish being sought. Generally 30 or 40-pound-test mono will work fine for most inshore species lacking sharp teeth. For tarpon exceeding 60 pounds, most experienced anglers prefer 80 to 120-pound mono. For more detail on the proper use of tarpon leaders, refer to pages 129-131 of a companion volume in the Library, *Fly Fishing for Bonefish, Permit & Tarpon.*

As to length of the bite tippet, if you are seeking world records, IGFA rules require that the bite leader (and all knots are included) cannot exceed 12 inches. Also, the tippet length must be at least 15 inches. If you are not interested in records, make the tippet any length that pleases you. But this is important: *all bite leaders should be relatively short.* A heavy diameter mono or wire bite tippet will usually cause the fish to refuse to strike, so a short wire leader — 4 to 6 inches — is recommended. Wire leaders of more than 8 inches will cause many refusals, particularly in clear water. However, on northern pike, which have a huge mouth and tend to over-run the fly, I will opt for a 10 to 14-inch wire leader. Pike are the dominant predator in their realm and they are rarely leader shy.

OVERLEAF: *Fishing in Grand Teton National Park, Wyoming.*

There are two ways to build a leader with a bite tippet. For many fishing situations, all you will need to do is simply build a basic tapered leader, following the formula I already discussed, to which you then add a short bite leader. There are several methods of doing this. The simplest way is to tie a very small barrel swivel (use a black one — the fish often will strike a bright silver swivel) to the tapered leader tippet, and then attach the bite tippet to the other eye of the barrel swivel. For this attachment, a simple Clinch Knot works just fine, particularly when you are adding mono of 80-pound test or larger. The disadvantage of this connection is that the swivel is visible, and in clear waters it can sometimes deter a fish from striking. But it does have one special advantage for certain situations. For example, I always use this type of rig when I am fishing the flats for bonefish or permit, using a basic tapered leader. But I want to be able to convert my rig very quickly to cast to the barracuda that also inhabit this type water. So in advance of my fishing, I will tie a few cuda patterns onto one end of a short length (4 to 5 inches) of wire, tie a tiny barrel swivel onto the other end, and put them in my fishing vest. When I spot a barracuda, I simply clip off my bonefish or permit fly, quickly tie the barrel swivel onto my leader, and I am ready to cast. Since cuda flies work best when well activated, the short length of wire doesn't seem to deter strikes — and wire is necessary, of course, to handle sharp teeth. Monofilament makes a poor bite leader for cudas.

SPECIAL SALTWATER LEADER
WITH BITE TIPPET

The tippet is the weakest part of any leader. If a bite tippet is added, almost any knot used to connect the two will mean a loss in tippet strength. For that reason *a special technique is*

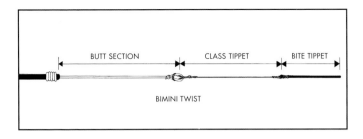

Leader with Bite Tippet

needed to add a bite tippet to a leader that is not tapered and still have a tippet that retains full-line strength.

Here is the generally accepted method: Start with a butt section of your choice (generally 60, 40, or 30-pound-test mono) and attach it to the fly line with a connection you prefer. Then tie a Surgeon's Loop or Non-Slip Mono Loop in the other end of the butt section. Next, take a length of tippet material (generally about 6 to 7 feet in length) and build Bimini Twists in each end. Now make a Surgeon's Loop or a Non-Slip Mono Loop in each of the Biminis. Loop one end of the Bimini Twist to the loop in the butt section. Connect the Bimini Twist on the other end to the bite leader — with either an Albright Knot or a Huffnagle Knot (if you are using mono for the bite leader), or an Albright Knot (if braided wire is used). If solid wire is utilized, make an Albright in the wire, and finish the connection by building a Haywire Twist (see tying instructions on pages 117-118), against the Albright Knot.

CONNECTING THE BITE LEADER TO THE FLY

There are several knots that can be used to attach the fly to the bite leader. Whenever full action of the fly is a must or helpful, then some type of loop knot should be considered.

This is especially important when fishing popping bugs, or when you have a smaller fly attached to heavy monofilament and you want the fly to dance a bit on the retrieve.

If mono is used as a bite leader, a Three-Turn Clinch Knot works well (see page 158 of *American Masters Fly Fishing Symposium: Volume II — Tackle* for tying instructions). This is preferred by many giant tarpon anglers when using heavy mono for the bite leader. Others prefer the Nail Knot, which holds the fly so that it never cocks in flight or on the retrieve.

If a loop knot is needed in a monofilament bite leader, there are three that will answer the need. The old standby, the Homer Rhode Loop Knot, has been used for generations (see pages 168-169 of *American Masters Fly Fishing Symposium: Volume II — Tackle* for tying instructions); or — and perhaps the most superior in terms of line strength — the Non-Slip Mono Loop; or — one that is favored by many great fly fishermen — the Uni-Knot (the Duncan Loop). All three of these knots work well for attaching the fly to the bite leader.

If you are using braided wire, you can attach the fly with a Figure 8 Knot. While this knot seems fragile, it is very strong, and is maybe the fastest knot you can tie, other than an Overhand Knot. You can also use braided wire to build a Homer Rhode Loop Knot or a Non-Slip Mono Loop (with only one turn required around the standing line). A loop knot in wire often improves the action of flies — especially popping bugs.

If you are using solid wire, there is only one knot that is regarded by most experienced anglers as being the proper one to use — the Haywire Twist. Many people make this knot improperly. Merely spiraling the tag end around the standing wire will not do it. Under fighting pressure this knot will frequently unwind, allowing the fish to escape. *It is important that 3 1/2 turns in an "X" shape be made before you spiral the standing end to finish the wraps.* Also, it is important to never cut the standing end, as this will leave a very sharp end that is liable to slice through your flesh. Instead, follow instructions for this knot, and after making a handle, bend it back and forth until it breaks. This leaves a smooth end.

Haywire Twist

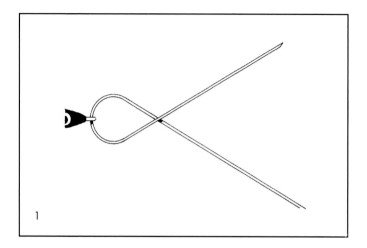

Step 1) Insert the solid trolling wire through the hook eye.

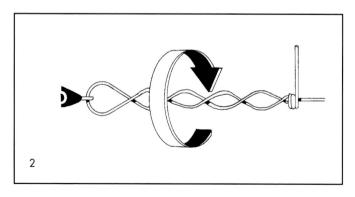

Step 2) Form three or four "Xs" with the wire as shown here.

Again, it is important that you do not spiral the wire around the standing line, but make these Xs. (Some people find it helpful to hold the wire immediately in front of the hook eye with a pair of needlenose pliers as the Xs are formed.)

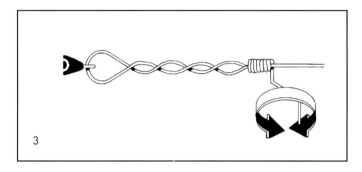

Step 3) Then, make four or six wraps with the tag end around the standing wire. It is essential that these wraps be made very close together!

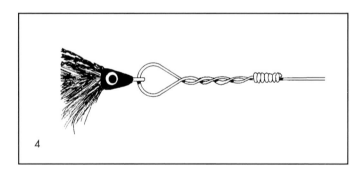

Step 4) Create a handle with the tag end of the wire, as shown here. Then, if you have the wraps close together, by rocking the handle back and forth the wire will break off, leaving a smooth, rounded end. *Never cut the tag end off with pliers.* This will leave a sharp edge that can cut you.

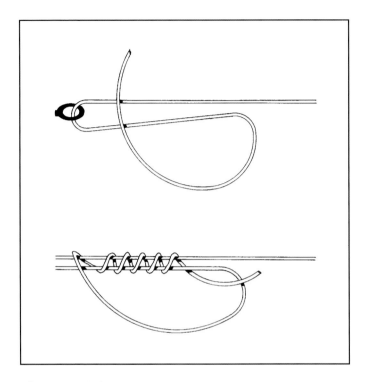

The Uni-Knot

Another excellent way for securing a leader to a fly is using a connection with two Uni-Knots (see above illustration) and some Powergum. As I discussed on pages 115-116 in *Fly Fishing for Trout, Volume I,* Powergum is a material that looks a lot like monofilament, but it differs in that it stretches like a rubber band. So, Powergum positioned in your leader acts like a shock absorber, preventing any sudden jerk occurring in the line that might diminish your chances of landing a big fish. While this Powergum technique was developed for trout fishing, it is an excellent connection for saltwater anglers whose game is seeking big fish on light tippets.

The Powergum strand is always placed in the butt section approximately 12 inches forward of a Nail Knot connecting the butt section of the fly line. Once installed in the butt section, the Powergum should not be any longer than about 6 inches. To connect the Powergum in the leader butt, simply use two Uni-Knots.

Cut a length of Powergum about 12 inches long. Hold the butt section and one end of the Powergum in the right hand. Curl the end of the Powergum and make a Uni-Knot. Make another Uni-Knot to connect the other end of the Powergum to the forward portion of the butt section. Because the Powergum is like a rubber band, you want to insure that the knot is firmly closed. Be sure to trim all ends as close as possible.

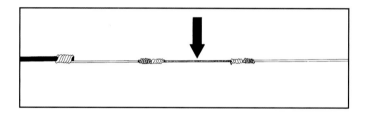

Use of Powergum

A fish can jerk against this section with little chance of breaking it. Important: Powergum is rubbery and stretches easily, so conventional knots won't work with this material — you must use the two Uni-Knot configuration.

ADDING DROPPERS TO THE LEADER

Trout fishermen often want to cast more than one fly on a leader. As many as three flies may be used at a time. This means that somehow, the angler must be able to attach the flies to

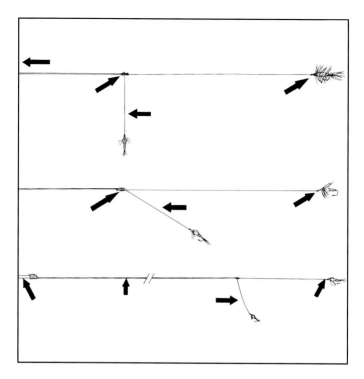

How the Blood Knot and the Surgeon's Knot are Used to Make a Dropper

the leader. The extension of the mono off the main leader is called a "dropper." There are all sorts of methods of doing this, but two work well and both are quick and easy to do.

The most important factor when constructing a dropper is to keep in mind that droppers that are too long will constantly tangle in your main leader, ruining the presentation. After many years of using droppers, I am convinced that the best dropper length is about the width of a man's hand, or approximately 4 inches from the position on the main leader where the dropper knot has been tied. If it's a little shorter, that doesn't seem to deter strikes. But, if the leader exceeds 5 inches, tangles will almost always result.

To build a dropper, simply clip the leader at the point where you want to install it. Then, use a Blood Knot or Surgeon's Knot to re-attach the two. *But, make sure that the standing end portion of monofilament to which you want to attach the fly protrudes outward from the leader when the knot is finished. Tie your fly to this protruding longer length of mono, and trim the other end of the mono close to the knot.* In the illustration on the previous page, at top is shown how the Blood Knot can be used to make a dropper. The middle rig shows how a Surgeon's Knot can be used to make a dropper. And at bottom, the illustration shows a completed rig with a Nail Knot on the fly line and the leader with a dropper.

Method of Tying Clinch Knots to a Two-Fly Indicator Rig

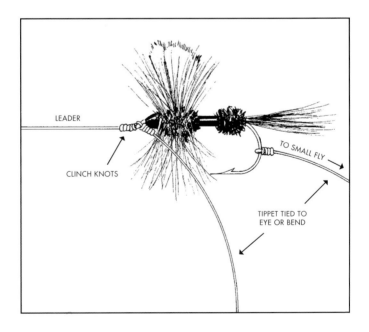

As Larry Tullis points out on pages 97-98 in his book in the Library, *Fly Fishing for Trout, Volume III,* another popular way to add a nymph dropper to an indicator dry fly — the guides in New Zealand have been doing this for years — is to tie from 6 to 60 inches of mono (the exact length being dictated by the depth of the water you are fishing) to the hook eye or bend of the dry fly with an Improved Clinch Knot.

INDEX